The Red & White Springs of Avalon

A Guide to the Healing Waters of Glastonbury

Nicholas R. Mann & Philippa Glasson

First published by The Temple Publications 01/06/2010

The Temple Publications Ltd.
Somerset
United Kingdom
www.thetemplepublications.co.uk
Email: info@thetemplepublications.co.uk

ISBN 978-0-9557400-7-7

Reprinted 2012

Cover design by Nicholas Mann
Page set up and preparation The Temple Publications
Printed in the United Kingdom by Quorum Print Services, Cheltenham

Contents

The Isle of Avalon lies in southwest Britain and was once almost entirely surrounded by the marshes and waters of an inland sea.

The Tor viewed from the west.

The Sacred Isle

Between Chalice Hill and the Tor on the Isle of Avalon, there once existed a small but exquisite valley, full of trees, into which flowed and blended two very distinctive springs. One of these springs flowed through a grove of yews and covered everything it touched with a blood-red, iron deposit. The other spring emerged from a cave in a small, verdant coombe and its waters released a white calcium deposit. Because of their colour, these waters were known as the Blood Spring and the White Spring, identifying them with a symbolism that has resonated throughout the history and mythology of Britain.

Today, the Blood or the Red Spring is restored and its waters flow through a pleasant series of pools and gardens. Since 1958 it has been in the care of Chalice Well Trust, whose goal is the "preserving of the well and surrounding land so that it will continue as a sacred shrine for all to visit and receive nourishment." The White Spring was not so fortunate—until recently. A large stone reservoir was imposed upon the site in the 1870s to supply water to the town of Glastonbury. Now in the care of the White Spring Trust, its interior has been redesigned to channel the waters into a central pool, and it too is open to all who wish to experience its unique properties. A wall and a road, Well House Lane, divide the two springs, preventing their waters from flowing together—as they must once have done—in a single natural stream.

The springs rise closely together and share the same source in the remarkable Tor that towers above them, yet they have a completely dissimilar mineral character. They have been distilled at different stages in the hydrological process taking place within the hill. According to geologists, the water of the springs cannot come from deep within the earth, as the whole of the Isle of Avalon rests upon a layer of impervious clay. Their water comes instead from rain that falls upon the slopes of the Tor and percolates into a subterranean aquifer at its core. This aquifer, fashioned over hundreds of millions of years (and responsible for the aquiform contours of the Tor itself), distills the two springs in a manner akin to the processes taking place in the retorts of the alchemists.

This small book explores the spiritual meaning of these extraordinary waters flowing out of Glastonbury Tor. It explains their relationship to Celtic legends of sacred cauldrons and wells, as well as their connection with the red and white elixirs produced in the alchemical work. The chemical wedding' or *coniunctio* of these substances produces the 'Philosophers' Stone,' a symbol often compared to the Holy Grail. The goal of alchemy is to purify the base metal of the lower mind and body, into the refined gold of spirit.

This purification takes place over the course of various distillations, described by different colours: the black, the white, the red. The struggle and suffering endured by the Grail knight or alchemist reflects the experience of many who come to Glastonbury today.

A couple unite in the alchemical retort, the alembic. *At this initial* coniunctio *in the* opus, *the alchemists' 'Great Work,' the couple have purified and grounded themselves so that spirit can take root and grow. From* Anatomiae auri sive tyrocinium medico-chymicum, *Johann Daniel Mylius, Frankfort, 1628.*

Approaching the Isle

When visitors came to the Isle of Avalon, they entered a sacred landscape. Coming by boat across the calm waters of the marshy inland sea, or crossing the causeway from the mainland to the east, they passed through a boundary that left the ordinary world behind. They came to a symbolic world centre: a place where the Tor as *axis mundi*, a world axis, joined the ordinary world with regions above and below. Around this cosmic axis turned the heavenly constellations, whose imprint, some traditions say, was made upon the surrounding land.

In the pre-Christian British tradition, Avalon was called *Ynys Witrin* or the 'Isle of Glass.' Set in the heart of the 'Summer Lands'—hence the name Somerset—it was regarded as an 'Isle of the Dead' or rather, an 'Isle of the Blest' where the souls of the deceased went for perpetual feasting, play and sport before rebirth. These departed souls ate the fruits of the Summer Lands, including the apple (Welsh: *aballon*), from which derives the name of Avalon. Early written sources such as *Cormac's Glossary* describe a Celtic doctrine of reincarnation or metempsychosis, in which souls passed freely from the world of the living to the world of the dead and back again. These sources always featured an island in the west. On this island, with its special trees, stood a prominent hill crowned with an Otherworldly dwelling. This was the *rath* of the fairy king or queen, variously called *Caer Sidi*, the spiral castle of the goddess Arianrhod; *Caer Wydr*, the glass castle; or *Caer Peredur*, the revolving castle. The castle had an entranceway through which it was possible—although not always easy—to pass. A guardian might appear and at once reveal, and obstruct, the way.

Up to and including the coming of Christianity, those who dwelt upon the island did only that which preserved or enhanced the original sacred order. They constructed a great ditch and bank across the eastern causeway, a *temenos* that divided and protected the island within from the ordinary land without. They sculpted the Tor over millennia to emphasise its cardinal nature, and finally they built a great mound from which they could watch the turning of the sun, the moon and the constellations in relation to the sacred isle. When the Christians came, they were so struck by the ancient sanctity of the place that they built a wealthy and extremely powerful abbey upon the island. Glastonbury Abbey, claiming to be the "First Church" founded in Britain, if not in Europe, possessed many rare treasures. The monks even claimed that their Saviour had sanctified the island with a visit as a boy.

Over time, the island, the Tor and its springs, its trees and portals, entered into the stories, visions and myths of the land itself. "Upon this Isle of Apples," William Camden wrote in the sixteenth century, "the fields require no rustic hand, but Nature only cultivates the land." It was seen as an earthly paradise, replete with great wonders and treasures, a mirror of heaven on earth. Perhaps above all, both Celtic myth and Christian legend hinted that it was here that King Arthur—the British 'Bear' King—slept in the Otherworld, awaiting the urgent call for his awakening in defence of the land.

The Red and White Springs, emerging out of their never-failing, world-mountain source, added to the potency of this extraordinary otherworldly landscape. The great mysteries of life and death, of the divine masculine and feminine, of queenship and kingship, the nature of goddess and god, and of the journey between this world and the next—are all evoked by the striking polarity of the two springs. Through them, the pilgrim can connect with powerful initiatory symbols: the Philosopher's Stone, the Holy Grail, the Cauldrons of Plenty and of Rebirth, and Excalibur, the Sword of Sovereignty. Most importantly of all, the Entrance to the Otherworld was said to be located on this "Fortunate Isle," the mysterious "Isle of Glass" that became known as Avalon.

The Ancient *Nemeton & Axis Mundi*

The valley of the two springs is located in the centre of a rich and unusual environment. Prior to the long process of draining the Somerset Levels, the Isle of Avalon lay in a tidal inland sea, surrounded by dense reed beds and freshwater marshes, and accessed only by boat or by the causeway which connected it to the mainland to the east. The original boundary of the island was defined by the highest floods and tides. Out of this flat and marshy landscape rose the group of hills which formed the island. Above them, dramatically dominating the entire area, rose the Tor—a West Country name for a high hill usually crowned with a rocky outcrop.

There is considerable evidence of prehistoric occupation in the area. From the evidence of Neolithic raised wooden trackways it is clear that people took advantage of the rich resources of the inland sea from an extremely early time. Many settlements have been found nearby, notably the Iron Age lake villages and trading places. But while ancient peoples frequently visited and shaped the island throughout prehistory, there is little evidence as yet that they actually lived upon it. So why did they come? What did they do on the island, and what was the significance to them of the fertile valley with its two springs?

The first man-made feature to consider is Ponter's Ball. This is a ditch and bank over three-quarters of a mile (1200m) in length that cuts across the eastern causeway to the mainland. It once made Avalon a true island. The name 'Ponter's Ball' originates from *pontis vallum*, Latin for the 'bridge over the ditch,' but the Abbey monks who named it and used it as a point of entry from the west did not build the earthwork. Excavations have indicated the most likely date of construction was the Iron Age, 800-100 B.C.E. Equivalent ditches in the Celtic world usually controlled important routes or defended territories. New Ditch, for example, across the Polden Ridge to the south of the island, near Dundon hill fort, defined tribal boundaries, defended against incursion, and controlled the movement of herds of cattle. But there is no hill fort and no great area of pasture on the island itself. Celtic activity in the region—the Lake Villages, the iron-working areas and trading routes, plus the settlements that ringed the inland sea—all relied upon the use of boats or used the Polden Ridge, bypassing the island. The marshy sea around the island seemingly formed a liminal zone, a rich but uncertain region on the boundaries of several tribes. Although the Celts evidently valued the island and may have felt it worthy of demarcation, few seem to have lived upon it. It is therefore possible that Ponter's Ball was built sometime earlier, during the Bronze Age or even the Neolithic.

The second feature for consideration are the enigmatic terraces carved upon the Tor. They represent enormous amounts of labour and are very difficult to date. Although there is pollen evidence of trees on the Tor in prehistory and in the early medieval period, this does not prove that the Tor was always covered in trees; instead, it is likely that trees have come and gone from the Tor over several periods. Furthermore, the terraces cannot have been created exclusively for agriculture. The monks of the Abbey and of St. Michael's Monastery on the Tor could have enhanced pre-existing terraces—especially to suggest a seven-tiered Calvary Mount, common in Europe in the middle ages—and they undoubtedly used the lower, southern-facing terraces for crops, but using the high, north-facing terraces on the Tor for cultivation is unheard of. This rules out an entirely agricultural explanation. Apart from the St Michael church on its summit, if the terraces can be shown either to be part of a Calvary Mount or to be prehistoric, we would have evidence that early people saw the Tor itself as some kind of sacred or ritual monument. But so far no conclusive excavation of the terraces has been conducted, nor any firm evidence produced from prehistory—until now.

The third and final feature for consideration is a large earthen mound located on the fourth and least well known of Avalon's hills, St. Edmund's or Windmill Hill. The Mound, as it is known locally, is shown on early maps of Glastonbury and is clearly present in early aerial photographs. Although affected by nurseries, windmills and the building of a council estate, the Mound still stands a few meters high and forty metres across. The most likely date for mounds of this type is around 2,000 B.C.E.; there are other examples in the area. Such mounds often have an astronomical purpose—an obsession of the Neolithic and Bronze Age peoples—and the Mound on Windmill Hill is seemingly no exception, since the observer standing on the Mound at sunrise on or close to the Winter Solstice will see the sun roll up the steep slope of the northern flank of the Tor. If the Mound can be shown to have been deliberately located upon Windmill Hill as a viewing point for astronomical events, it would tell us a great deal about how prehistoric people viewed the Tor.

In conclusion, as there is little evidence of any practical reason for the construction of Ponter's Ball, it is possible to conclude that it was built to form a sacred enclosure called by the Greeks a *temenos* and the Celts a *nemeton.* This earthwork created a ritual boundary separating the mundane world from the sanctified land within. In the same manner, the terraces on the Tor were plausibly intended to enhance its impact as the world mountain, while the Mound was apparently built to observe the heavens turning around the Tor's summit. This evidence suggests that the Isle of Avalon was deemed to be a sacred place from at least the time when Ponter's Ball, the Tor terraces and the Mound were first made. This early reverence was continued in subsequent ages by those—including Lake Villagers, Romans, 'Dark Age' landlords and the Abbey—who felt it worthwhile to maintain the highly significant, but practically inefficient boundary, and also to build magnificent religious structures upon the Tor and the Abbey site.

An engraving of Glastonbury, by Hollar after Dugdale, 1654. The Tor and its terraces are prominent and just to the left of centre, a windmill sits on the mound on St. Edmund's Hill.

Here the royal couple, identified with sun and moon, engage in a purifying bath. Philosophia reformata, *Johann Daniel Mylius, Frankfort, 1622.*

The Avalon Traditions

From this evidence a picture begins to emerge of how the Isle of Avalon was regarded in prehistory. The natural and manmade features of the island created the feeling of a place set apart from the normal scope of life. It was a sacred isle, a *nemeton*, defined by a ritual boundary. With no regular inhabitants, the island was seen as a Paradise realm where the divine or otherworldly powers were honoured. As *axis mundi*, a world axis, the Tor formed a connection between the above and the below, around which earth and sky turned. It served as the point of focus for the four cardinal and the two vertical directions. At its centre was the symbolic opening through which the traveller between the worlds could pass. From this opening flowed the two springs, one red, one white, representing the fundamental polarity of the earthly realm. A viewing platform, a great mound, was constructed upon the island to observe and mark the most auspicious times in the fluctuation of the great cosmic cycles. The implicit invitation to the Avalonian pilgrim was to be guided by this sacred geography towards a profound understanding of the place of humans within the cosmos.

When these natural and man-made features are considered in their entirety, they reveal that the Isle of Avalon possesses an extraordinary *genius loci*, a 'spirit of place' with a singular purpose and an unique function. This is a place where the veil between the worlds, between the solar, the terrestrial and the *daemonic* realms, dissolves; a place where the *anima mundi,* or world soul, connects with the life of the individual soul to provide healing and initiation. The truth of this is attested by the life-changing experiences of many who come here today.

The Divine Feminine & the Waters of Avalon

> In ancient times Logres was a rich country but it was turned into a Wasteland for the kingdom lost the voices of the wells and the maidens that were in them. These maidens would offer food and drink to wayfarers. A traveller had only to wish for food and seek out one of the wells and a maiden would appear from out of the well with the food he liked best, a cup of gold in her hand. No wayfarers were excluded from this service.
>
> From *The Elucidation: a Prologue to the Conte del Graal.*

The writer of *The Elucidation,* a 13th century French commentary on the Grail romance, described how the ruler of Logres or Britain, was bound to protect the maidens of the wells. But King Amangon broke this custom: "Although it was his duty to guard the damsels and keep them within his peace, he raped one of them and took away her golden cup for his own service." He and his men did the same elsewhere, until "no damsel was seen issuing from a well… and the service of the wells ceased."

According to the extremely ancient traditions of the British isles, ancient wells were not just precious sources of water but also places where tutelary goddesses preside over powers of abundance and sovereignty. Celtic rites of sovereignty were conducted beside sacred rivers, lakes and pools. In Celtic tradition, a man became king by marrying a representative of the goddess of the land, who often appeared beside a spring. The Isle of Avalon was purportedly the place where Excalibur, the sword of King Arthur was made and guarded by one such goddess. After initially being drawn from a stone, it was re-presented to Arthur by its otherworldly guardian, the 'Lady of the Lake,' who can therefore be understood as a 'maiden of the springs of Avalon.' Eventually, Excalibur was returned to the waters of the island. But this was only after Arthur's knights had set out on their greatest quest: to find the golden cup, the Holy Grail that healed the Wasteland. By describing the knights' goal as the restoration of the maidens to the holy wells, the

Elucidation repeats the familiar Grail theme of mending the broken relationship between humanity and the land—a quest in which reconnection with the Divine Feminine is central.

Gwynn ap Nudd & the Sublunary Sphere

According to Somerset tradition an important entrance to the Otherworld, the Celtic realm of Annwn, is located on the Tor. Its male guardian is Gwynn ap Nudd, the Lord of the Underworld. Gwynn is a *psychopomp*, guide for the dead, and a King of Faery. He presides over the otherworld realm of Annwn (literally 'not world'). His father Nudd or Nodens is another ancient British deity of the Underworld and tutelary deity of the River Severn. Celtic tradition saw both Nudd and Gwynn, 'White Son of Night'—which suggests the moon—as guides between this world and the next. In Welsh legend, Gwynn helps King Arthur hunt a great boar, *Twrch Trwyth*, but in Scotland, Gwynn and Arthur dissolve into one and the same person. Both stem from the same archetype of the hero or king asleep in a cave below a hollow hill.

British folklore has many references to fairy riders and fairy hunts, it also tells of departing souls being gathered up by a legendary group of riders called the Wild Hunt; in the West country this troupe of spirits is led by Gwynn, accompanied by hounds and other huntsmen and women. Leaders of this hunt elsewhere reputedly include Herne, Herle, Wotan, Odin, Arthur, Diana, and the Fairy Queen. Both the hunt's 'Hounds of Hell,' the *Cwm Annwn,* and their horses are sometimes described as red and white. When the Celtic king Pwyll makes his journey into Annwn, as described in the Welsh *Mabinogion*, not only are the creatures he meets there coloured red and white, so are the clothes and furnishings of the people.

The Fairy Queen has a complementary and equally important role to that of Gwynn in the folklore of Avalon. According to Giraldus Cambrensis and Geoffrey of Monmouth, both writing in the twelfth century, the island was the abode of Morgan le Fey ('the Fairy')—an aspect of the Divine Feminine intimately concerned with the Otherworld, and the processes of death and rebirth. She is described in Arthurian romance as living in a house of glass, a sun-chamber on which all the rays of the sun converged. In Avalonian tradition, Morgan le Fey escorted the dead over the glassy waters of the surrounding inland sea; this may account for the ancient name of Glass-town-bury, *Ynys Witrin* the 'Isle of Glass.' It was Morgan who received the dying Arthur on the Isle of Avalon, to prepare him for his journey into the next world.

When the soul entered the Celtic Underworld it did not remain there for long. According to many accounts of the journey to the Otherworld, a magical vessel or cauldron appeared, immersion in which ensured rebirth. After the appropriate length of time in Annwn, partaking in the perpetual 'Feast of Age,' the Celts said the soul either resumed its life in another body, or moved to occupy some other form, possibly quite an abstract one. For some, however, such as the Welsh bard Taliesin, it was possible to visit the otherworld and return in the same body, hopefully wiser for the experience. This is a form of the initiatory journey.

The Glastonbury literature reports that as the entranceway to the Otherworld, Avalon not only received King Arthur but was, according to Melkin, also "hungry for the death of pagans." Thought to be a sixth-century bard, Melkin anticipated a time when the ancient spiritual power of the island could be restored. Christian literature about Avalon also furnishes us with the legend of St. Collen, who came to Glastonbury in the seventh century. After serving as Abbot, Collen retired for a life of contemplation in a cell beside a spring at the foot of the Tor. From here he was conducted into the Underworld, where he met Gwynn and banished the Lord of Annwn from this world with holy water. The St. Collen legend is obviously an account of an exorcism—but exorcism of exactly what?

Such traditions suggest that the Tor has long been seen as the place where a balance could be weighed between opposing principles or pairs of antagonists. The experience of polarity, whether between a dual male or dual female principle, or between male and female, is characteristic of what Renaissance thinkers called the 'sublunary sphere': the mundane, terrestrial sphere, or literally, everything 'under the moon.' Alchemical teachings suggest that the Red and White Springs represent and focus this polarity in the physical realm. We can trace aspects of such polarity in stories that pair and oppose Gwynn and Arthur, Morgan and Arthur, the fairy king and Guinevere.

In the Welsh *Mabinogion,* Gwynn has another male counterpart, Gwythyr ap Greidyawl, with whom he is locked in a perpetual cosmic conflict in relation to an aspect of the Divine Feminine:

> Creiddylad daughter of Llud Silver Hand, the most majestic woman ever in Britain or the three islands; for her Gwythyr son of Greidyawl and Gwynn son of Nudd fight every May Day until the Judgment… Creiddylad had gone to Gwythyr, but before he could sleep with her Gwynn came and carried her off by force. Gwythyr collected an army and went to fight Gwynn, but Gwynn conquered… When Arthur heard of this he called on Gwynn… and peace was made between Gwynn and Gwythyr. Creiddylad was left in the house of her father undisturbed by either side, and every May Day the two men would fight…

Gwythyr ap Greidyawl has a heavenly, solar origin, quite unlike the earthy and lunar character of Gwynn, while Creiddylad emerges as a Persephone figure journeying around the cycle of the year. This is a cosmology where her two suitors divide the cycle of time and the cosmos into two parts, while she represents an underlying unity. This theme is repeated exactly in a sixth-century manuscript when Caradoc of Llancarfan describes how the solar king, Arthur, has to rescue Queen Guinevere from the lunar king, Melwas—the

the Cornish name of the fairy king—who has imprisoned her in Glastonbury Tor, apparently as the embodiment of the power of sovereignty.

The alchemical *opus* sought to resolve the red and white polarity both in the soul and in matter, providing access to deep levels of healing and to subtle spiritual forces usually seen as solar, lunar or stellar. By working in the landscape, alchemists sought to resolve in one realm the analogous polarities of another, restore the lost balance between inner and the outer worlds and avoid the dualism present in Christianity and Gnosticism, where one term in the polarity is valued above the other. The Christian tradition reveals a determination to cleanse the Tor of previous associations and practices. Both the exorcism by St. Collen and the dedication of the Tor to St. Michael were attempts to restructure and redirect the alchemical and geomantic possibilities of the sacred isle, by placing its healing sanctuaries, initiations, and traffic between the worlds under the aegis of Christ.

Stained glass in St. John's Church, Glastonbury, showing Joseph of Arimathea bringing the two cruets containing the blood and water from Christ's wounds to Glastonbury.

Joseph of Arimathea & the Holy Grail

All subsequent Glastonbury traditions built upon these ancient pagan foundations, perhaps most elaborately in the legend of the coming of Joseph of Arimathea. The legend claims that Joseph travelled to Glastonbury from Palestine, via southern France and Cornwall, carrying with him two cruets and the Holy Grail—the cup used by Christ at the Last Supper. These cruets, usually depicted as red and white, were said to have contained the blood and the water that issued from Christ's wounds at his crucifixion. After the miracle of the blossoming thorn staff planted on Wearyall Hill, Joseph was said to have remained in Avalon, built the "First Church"—the first church in Britain, if not the world—and buried the Grail and two cruets in the vicinity of Chalice Hill. From "that day forth," local tradition says, the spring which rose at the foot of Chalice Hill "flowed red with the healing blood of Christ."

The Joseph legend is central to Glastonbury's claim to be a very early, if not the earliest, British Christian foundation. This claim later made the Abbey a highly popular place of pilgrimage, enjoying great power and wealth until the dissolution of the monasteries by Henry VIII. Whatever the historic truth of the legend, it is remarkable for the structural consistency it shares with the older traditions. It is possible to imagine early Christians arriving at the long established sanctuary of Avalon and finding a local cult instituted upon a sacred mountain—involving precise astronomical observation, a doctrine of reincarnation, various special trees or the one World Tree, a red and a white spring, a cauldron of rebirth, and an entranceway to the Underworld guarded by powerful male and female deities. The Christians would have required both a rededication of the springs and a strong alternative myth to incorporate this powerful cult into their religion. While the legend of Joseph with his staff, cup and two cruets provides us with just such a myth of incorporation, it also reveals the very ancient and powerful symbols it was intended to conceal.

The Red "chymical powder" of Dr. Dee & Edward Kelley

Dr. John Dee, Renaissance magus and scholar, communicator with angels, mathematician, astrologer and physician to Queen Elizabeth I, felt a close connection with Glastonbury, where he believed King Arthur to have been buried. In the seventeenth century it was reported that in 1583 Dee's magical assistant and 'scryer', Edward Kelley, had found a book by St. Dunstan, Glastonbury's most famous abbot, with an accompanying map, hidden among the ruins of Glastonbury Abbey. With its aid, Kelley claimed to have found in the Abbey grounds a red "chymical powder" of St. Dunstan, who is often suggestively described as a 'blacksmith'. This was reputedly the Philosophers' Stone—the much sought-after alchemical elixir that turned base matter into gold. Dee and Kelley were said to have used this wonderful red transmuting powder to perform not just one but several alchemical demonstrations in which base metal was transmuted into gold. The influential seventeenth-century scholar Elias Ashmole reported that the powder used by Dee and Kelley was so potent that a "single ounce could produce 22,694 pounds of gold."

John Dee, Ashmolean Museum, Oxford.

As Dee himself acknowledged, alchemy was not just the search to turn base metal into gold, although that had its importance. It was also the means of transformation of the soul—or the distillation of *pneuma*, spirit, from soul—through a complex process of purification. Gold was the metaphor for discovering the true spiritual nobility of the soul as it passed through the challenges of the terrestrial or the sublunary sphere. At the same time, the physical reaction taking place in an appropriate vessel or retort served as an appropriate metaphor for the *coniunctio*—the union of polarities or opposites in what alchemists called the Royal Marriage. The base metal underwent purifying stages associated with the colours black, white, yellow and red. The red "chymical powder" or elixir found by Dee and Kelley was purportedly the result of the final stages of the Royal Marriage. Naturally, we can see why this wonderful substance would have been attributed to St. Dunstan, who as a 'blacksmith' and Abbot of great fame had the reputation of a successful alchemist who knew the secret of matter's transmutation.

The waters of life rise in a three-fold fountain between the polarities of the worldly realm. The fons mercurialis *from the* Rosarium philosphorum*, Frankfort, 1550.*

The symbolic associations with white and red—male and female, life and death, sun and moon etc.—can switch from one polarity to the other. This ambiguity shows that red blood can mean both life and death. Thus one of the heraldic devices of Glastonbury Abbey shows a pelican tearing at its chest, so it can feed its young directly with its blood. White can mean both death and being filled with light. Therefore we must look at the character of alchemical transformation itself and find a 'third force' that resolves dualism and material identification and makes soul healing and presence possible. The alchemists saw the soul's journey of healing, initiation and voyaging between the worlds into the divine realm of unification as ruled over by *Mercurius*—this was not just simply the slippery metal mercury, but also the divine hermaphrodite of many forms, who combined sexual polarities in a single being. To understand *Mercurius* meant being initiated into a more fundamental state of being, a withdrawal from the ego identified self in the world.

A Pelican, over the east gateway to Glastonbury Abbey, feeds its young with drops of blood from its chest. The Pelican symbolises an alchemical vessel and also represents the 'red elixir.'

The themes that recur throughout the Glastonbury legends reveal a consistent narrative that turns around a sacred landscape, a polarity of red and white, a mystical vessel of transformation, a world axis, and an Otherworld entrance with its guardians. The combined effects of this unique terrain conferred healing and spiritual enlightenment through specific symbols and initiations. The origin and ascription of these powerful symbols to Glastonbury is mainly due to the numinous atmosphere of the island itself with its world mountain and two springs. Those who discover the Avalonian springs can open a doorway to the resolution not just of the polarities within but also of those between the inner and the outer worlds.

A gateway at Chalice Well in King Arthur's Court. The flagstones preserve the lines of the eighteenth-century bathhouse. The sword of St. Michael crosses the two circles in the wrought ironwork over the gateway.

The Red Spring

An extremely complex subterranean system provides the water which rises under pressure in the spring at Chalice Well. The spring has a high chalybeate (iron) content, a constant temperature of 52 degrees F., (11 degrees C.,) and a rate of flow that varies from a peak of approximately 25,000 gallons per day (gpd), to a low of 18,000 gpd in a dry summer.

The Chalice Well Trust was founded in 1958 by Wellesley Tudor Pole O.B.E, a businessman who was also an extraordinary psychic and writer. Tudor Pole (b. 1884) made regular journeys, often in sleep, to what he called "*au dela*," the other side. There he would help souls in distress. His life included the finding of the cup supposedly used by Christ (a claim he was later to retract) and an unsuccessful quest for the lost Library of Alexandria. His friendship with powerful members of British society inspired the creation of the 'Silent Minute' during the Second World War. During this minute, while Big Ben struck 9 pm, many psychics attuned to the spirit of the land and visualised a light covering and protecting Britain. Dion Fortune (1890-1946), who made a home in Chalice Orchard, just above the White Spring, was greatly involved in this kind of occult work. Tudor Pole's friend and effective spiritual heir, Sir George Trevelyan, taught that a similar light, which he called 'the Christ,' had urgently to be anchored in the land as well as in individual bodies through working with the chakra system.

The magnificent pair of yew trees in Chalice Well Gardens.

Alice Buckton, a poet, potter, teacher and dramatist, owned the Chalice Well property from 1913 until her death in 1945. Tudor Pole was her original inspiration to come to Glastonbury. She later provided him with the vision of a Trust that made the establishment of Chalice Well his central focus in the later years of his life. Tudor Pole died in 1968, but Sir George battled on until 1996. The goal of these early 'light workers' was to restore the bond between spirit and matter, the sacred and the earth. This legacy continues to guide the work of the Chalice Well.

The Yew Trees

In the 1960s the Chalice Well Trust sponsored archaeological excavations that provided marginal evidence of prehistoric and Roman occupation, and showed that the yew trees in the garden had always been there. The archaeological evidence suggested that the source of the Red or the Blood Spring once flowed in a vivid red stream beside a large grove of yews. A stump of yew found eleven feet underground was dated to 300 C.E., or earlier. This demonstrated that parts of the valley floor had risen considerably over the years. Because of the challenges this presented, in addition to the buildings on the site, only a small amount of archaeological evidence was obtained.

In Celtic, classical and European tradition the yew tree is associated with death and rebirth. Its berries are toxic, the tree dark and often stained with red sap. It is possible for a yew to reach extreme old age; they have the greatest longevity of any European tree. The yew can achieve a massive girth and, when hollow, it can send new shoots upward from the centre of the tree. The observation of these qualities was probably responsible for the association of the tree with death and rebirth. Early Christian graveyards were either placed around ancient yews, or yews were planted in them; the tree was said to "send a root to the mouth of every corpse."

The Wellhead & the Vesica Piscis

The archaeologist Philip Rahtz found that the lower sides of the shaft in which the Red Spring rises were built from large blocks of stone without mortar. Rahtz proposed that the first structure on the site was a traditional freestanding medieval well house, built around 1200 CE, using stones from the Abbey Church, which had burnt down in 1184. He also thought that the five-sided, brick-roofed chamber to one side of the well shaft was a mid-eighteenth century addition, made when the well became enormously popular as a place of healing. Today the visitor at the wellhead looks into the well house through an opening made in the roof. Later excavation, however, showed that silting up around the wellhead was not as deep as Rahtz thought; the ground nearby shows undisturbed bedrock after a foot or two. The well house had been set mostly into the ground.

The wellhouse for the Red Spring may have looked like this around 1200 C.E., although recent evidence suggests it was set more deeply into the ground. Drawing by Alan Royce.

The geometrical figure known as the *vesica piscis* was first brought into the garden in the early twentieth century, when Frederick Bligh Bond, architect in charge of the restoration of the Abbey, designed a new lid for the well after the Great War. Bond found that the proportions of the *vesica piscis* often used in classical and Renaissance architecture were also present in the design of Glastonbury Abbey, particularly in the proportions of the Mary Chapel. He therefore incorporated this design into the lid. You can create the vesica by drawing two equal size circles, one on the circumference of the other. Its simple proportions embody all the ratios of sacred geometry, including *phi* (1:1.618'), the Golden Section. The *vesica piscis* has been described as a symbol of the merging of different traditions as well as the union of the polarities of spirit and matter, masculine and feminine. People from many different spiritual paths blessed the new lid in a ceremony held in 1919. Bligh Bond gave an address in which he described the figure as "the wound in the side of Jesus," the "radiance around the figure of Christ," and the "North and the invisible worlds." The huge slabs of stone that you can see around the well-head were also put in place at that time.

The Vesica Piscis on the lid of the Red Spring or Chalice Well.

The *vesica piscis* is a symbol of the creation and polarity of form in the world. At its centre lies the *aureole*, the *mandorla*, a yoni- or almond-shaped gateway of birth, creation, ecstasy and unity. The geometrical progression created by the *vesica piscis* unfolds endlessly in the inner dimensions, just as it unfolds endlessly in the external world. This simple symbol is therefore an expression of the ideal, unified proportions of the inner world emerging into time and form, and of the polarities of the outer world returning to the unconditioned and unified realm of the eternal.

The White Spring

When the building of a reservoir was proposed in 1872 to tap the waters of the springs that rose in the valley between Chalice Hill and the Tor, local antiquarians raised an outcry about the destruction of a beauty spot steeped in great historical and mythological interest. But the area was suffering from cholera outbreaks at that time and as the town council needed a safe source of water, construction of the reservoir went ahead. The original spring (or, as we shall see, the springs) emerged out of an opening about 90 feet back from the present lane and 20 feet above it in the direction of the Tor. The steep slopes of the coombe were covered by a profusion of ferns, mosses, lichens, ivy, shade and moisture-loving flowers and grasses. All around, beside little eddying and dripping pools, were bulbous forms created by the calcium in the water.

"What was Glastonbury like then?" wrote George Wright in 1896. "One thing that clings to me was the beautiful Well House Lane of those days, before it had been spoilt by the erection of the reservoir. …the lane itself was beautiful, for the whole bank was a series of fairy dropping wells—little caverns clothed with moss and verdure, and each small twig and leaf was a medium for the water to flow, drop, drop, drop, into a small basin below. This water contained lime, and pieces of wood or leaves subject to this dropping became encrusted with a covering of lime."

The White Spring as it may have been before the building of the reservoir.

The reservoir built in 1872 at the foot of Well House Lane.

The builders of the reservoir dug out the back of the coombe and installed a mixing chamber and a low, brick-lined tunnel that ends in a natural cave, the source of the White Spring. Full access into this cave system is now impossible due to what appears to be a fairly recent collapse of the roof. Judging from the high iron content of one of the springs in the mixing chamber, it appears that an offshoot from the Red Spring finds its way under Well House Lane to emerge beside the White Spring. This offshoot flows intermittently and deposits an extremely high concentration of iron. Two other springs are also intermittent and every indication points to these being groundwater filtered from the Tor. The mixing chamber served to separate the water of these springs from the more potable White Spring water, and only diverted them into the reservoir when demand required it.

It was not long, however, before a better water supply was found and by the end of the nineteenth century boreholes at West Compton, several miles to the east, met all Glastonbury's water needs. This water is still pumped up to reservoirs on the flanks of the Tor and should not be confused with the water of the local springs that originate under the Tor. In 1982, the Water Board sold the White Spring into private hands. The current owners have established the White Spring Trust, which permits access to the spring at regular times and encourages its use for ceremony and meditation. The Trust has developed the interior of the reservoir as a series of shrines to female and male deities, and recently commissioned John Martineau to design a central geometric pool as well as other pools in which ritual bathing is possible.

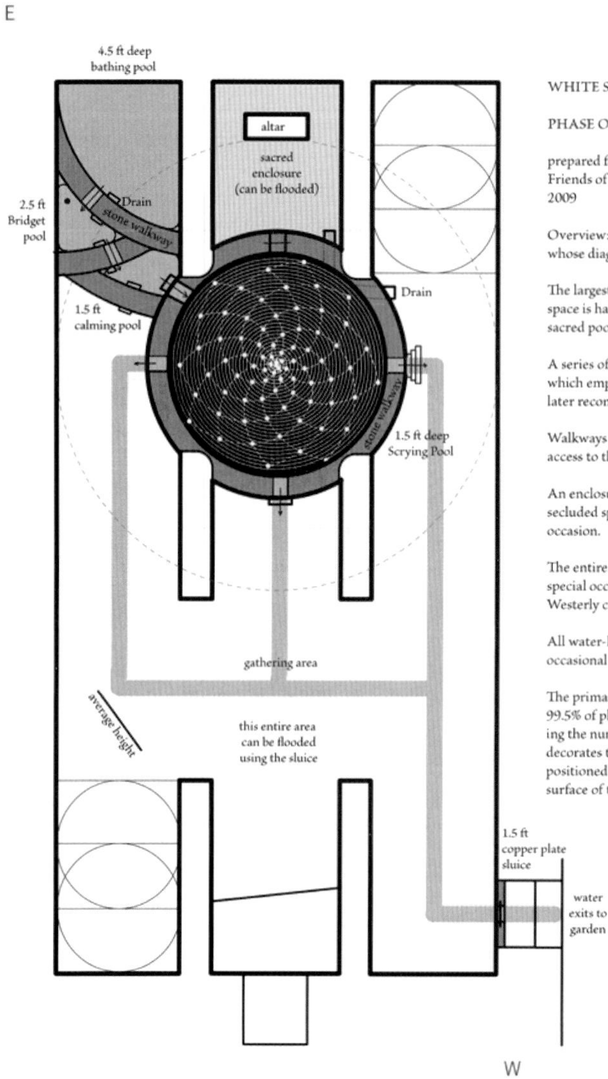

WHITE SPRING GLASTONBURY

PHASE ONE PLAN

prepared for the Trustees, Companions and Friends of the White Spring in February 2009

Overview: The building is a double square, whose diagonal is a precise East-West axis.

The largest circle that can be drawn in the space is half the width and shall form a sacred pool.

A series of smaller pools feeds the large pool which empties into three streams which later recombine as one.

Walkways surround the pool and allow access to the smaller pools.

An enclosure at the back provides a secluded space, which can be flooded on occasion.

The entire space can also be flooded for special occasions using a sluice in the Westerly corner.

All water-holding areas can be drained for occasional cleaning.

The primary phyllotaxis pattern, used by 99.5% of plants on Earth, and also embodying the numbers of the Moon and Venus decorates the floor of the pool as carefully positioned white stones, just under the surface of the water.

Design for the White Spring 2009. Reproduced with kind permission of John Martineau.

The plaque over the White Spring marking the year of its construction 1872.

The Source of the Waters

But where does the water of the two springs originate? White Spring water contains calcium, fluctuates quickly according to rainfall and emerges from the ground under little or no pressure. Red Spring water is rich in iron, fluctuates slowly and makes its way upward with significant force. A distant artesian origin for the Red Spring could account for the different qualities of the springs, and for their high position below a small rainfall catchment area. But while some think the water is of a distant or even a primary origin, emerging from the earth, the underlying Keuper Marl is a very poor carrier of water and effectively prevents any water rising from below.

The temperature of the water (11 degrees C.) is consistent with that of other local springs and makes a primary or 'juvenile' origin unlikely, as water coming from closer to the earth's core invariably has a higher temperature. As the surrounding geology does not support an artesian or a juvenile origin, and assuming the water from the two springs is of a local origin, the challenge is to explain why the Red Spring rises under pressure, why it is relatively constant, and why its mineral content differs from that of the White Spring when the available rainfall catchment area for both springs (Glastonbury Tor) is so small—and there is no iron in the area. Over the years, geologists and hydrologists have come forward to provide such an explanation.

A long time ago, what was to become this part of the world was an ocean floor receiving vast amounts of sediment. Over millions of years, thick and contrasting layers of sediment accumulated. On the bottom were the Lias beds laid down in the Jurassic age (208-146 million years ago). These included the Keuper Marl and the local limestone known as Blue Lias. Above these beds was deposited a layer of softer yellow stone, known as Midford Sandstone. It is this sandstone that forms the Tor. Above that were yet more layers, at least one of which contained huge quantities of iron.

As land masses shifted over the next hundred million years, all these layers lifted upwards to form a plateau. Heavy tropical rains falling on this plateau drained into the soft underlying stone, and water flowing downwards from the surface of the plateau carried the minerals from the upper layers into the lower. Over many millions of years the iron in the upper layers leached into the water to be deposited in the layers of sand and shale below. As the iron rich water passed into the Midford layers it hardened the sandstone, and sometimes caused even harder nodules to form. These nodules, or Tor Burrs, range in size from less than a centimetre to the metre-long 'egg stone' behind the Abbot's Kitchen in the Abbey grounds.

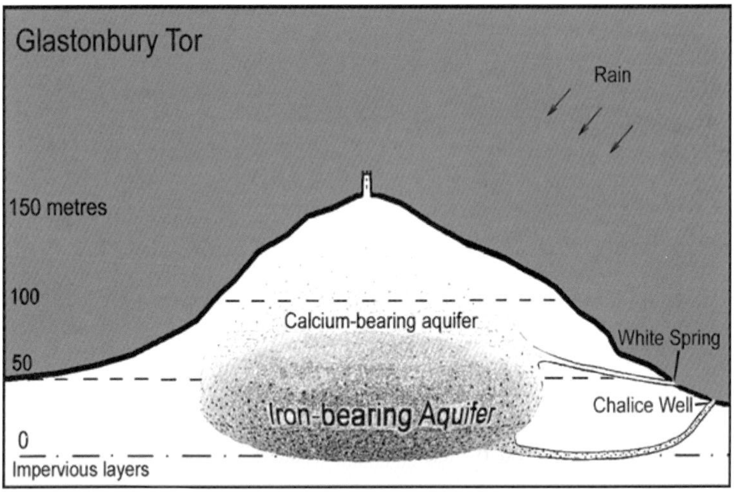

The aquifer within the Tor resembles a retort with an upper and a lower outlet. Heavy rain falling on the Tor fills the aquifer and rapidly increases the rate of flow of the White Spring. The rate of flow of the Red Spring remains relatively constant due to the volume of water in the aquifer as a whole, but it varies slightly on a seasonal basis—more in winter, less in summer.

Over time, according to this theory, erosion removed all the top layers of the Tor and began to penetrate the lower Midford Sandstone. Where the concentrated iron-rich water from earlier epochs had infiltrated and hardened the sandstone, however, it resisted erosion, and so the familiar landscape of the present day began to appear. Glastonbury Tor emerged, as the iron-impregnated and hardened sandstone that forms its core resisted erosion while the softer stone around it wore away. Within the Tor, however, remains an aquifer, a water-bearing system created in earlier times when large amounts of water filtered through from above. The bottom part of this aquifer, in the heavier and impervious shales and limestones, is heavily saturated with iron.

Rain falling on the Tor is sufficient to keep the aquifer saturated, and because of its size and the impervious clay below, the aquifer does not dry up.

When it rains on the Tor some water is discharged by surface springs, but much of the water finds its way into the aquifer. The top layers of the aquifer fill up and discharge their water—within a week or so—into the White Spring. During dryer times the water is discharged at a much slower rate of flow. The water picks up the calcium present in the limestone layers and deposits these at the White Spring. But the water that lies in the lower layers of the aquifer has a quite different character. As it passes through the denser sediment of the lower layers, the water picks up the iron present there, then emerges under the fairly constant artesian pressure, temperature and volume of the Chalice Well.

The Red Spring, although fed by the same aquifer, does not fluctuate like the White Spring, as its rate of flow is determined by the relatively stable volume of water in the aquifer as a whole. As the aquifer reaches maximum saturation in the winter months the volume of water increases slightly, however, while in the summer months it decreases. The maximum flow of the Chalice Well in winter is around 25,000 gpd, while in summer it falls to around 19,000 gpd. This is consistent with local rainfall patterns. Any further increase of pressure in the aquifer is also released by the offshoot of the Chalice Well above the White Spring reservoir. This slowly increases in flow during wet spells and ceases entirely during very dry weather.

Taking the average rainfall for Glastonbury to be twenty-six inches per year, and assuming the catchment area of the White Spring to be the Tor, or about one sixth of a square mile, then following the standard equation that allows for one half loss of this water by evaporation and run off, the maximum volume of water expected to issue from the area covered by the Tor is in the region of 125,000 gpd. This amount agrees with the average annual volume of the Chalice Well, 20,000 gpd, plus the average volume of the White Spring, 10,000 gpd (although it can be many times this), plus the other springs in the area, 90-100,000 gpd. Thus the catchment area formed by the Tor above the Red and White Springs is sufficient to supply their waters.

This explanation satisfactorily accounts for the origin, character, mineral nature and mineral differences between the Red and the White Springs. If true, the waters of the springs are, in effect, 'home brewed.' They do not originate from far away, but from an aquifer created in highly unusual conditions below the Tor. In fact, underground waters created the Tor and were responsible for the shape it has today.

The Subtle Energies of the Avalonian Alembic

The Tor is an iron-impregnated sandstone hill underlain by beds of limestone, marl and impervious clay. The whole contains a natural aquifer formed many millions of years ago, when there was ground overhead and mineral rich water

The royal couple, as Sol *and* Luna, *stand between a hill representing the 'Philosophers' Stone,' out of which flow water and fire. Mercurius stands uniting the two worlds—represented by two lions with a single stream flowing from its one mouth—while overhead turn seven heavenly spheres beginning with the zodiac. Detail of* Janitor pansophus, *fig. IV, Musaeum hermeticum, Frankfort, 1678.*

in the system. The upper part of this aquifer is a loose conglomerate of sandstone and limestone in which there are hardened Tor Burrs and whose water finds immediate release through the tunnels of the White Spring. Tremendous quantities of iron have leached into the lower part of the aquifer, whose water finds much slower and constant release at the Red Spring. With the erosion of the overlying land mass, the aquifer is now contained within—although on a much smaller scale—a hardened conical hill jutting above a surrounding plain. The aquifer and its layered minerals consequently form a core with highly unusual and subtle properties.

Several authors have described these properties. In 1968 the well known ley researcher and author John Michell showed how the St. Michael line that runs through the axis of the Tor mysteriously connected many ancient and sacred sites in Britain. In their best-selling 1995 publication, *The Sun and the Serpent*, dowsers Hamish Miller and Paul Broadhurst described the energies around the Tor as sections of two intertwining earth-currents they called the "Mary and Michael lines." The two lines spiral around the Tor in a manner congruent with the terraces, and thus with the enormous labyrinth described by the Arthurian scholar Geoffrey Ashe in his 1979 booklet *The Glastonbury Tor Maze*. In the 1930s and 40s, psychics such as Dion Fortune, Iris Campbell and Olive Pixley, referred to "glazed canopies," "spiral vortexes" and other subtle energies radiating out from the Tor. In 1987 the psychic Page Bryant described the Tor as a "combined magnetic and electrical vortex." Whatever we may think about the non-scientific approach of these authors, they generally encourage us to imagine the central axis of the Tor as a three-dimensional vortex that is either centrifugally spiralling in ever widening circles, or centripetally spiralling to a concentrated point of focus—perhaps both happening simultaneously to form a vortical sphere.

In *Energy Secrets of Glastonbury Tor*, Nicholas describes the employment of the vortex by nature for its wind, water and organic forms (you only have to think of the DNA spiral), while the spherical vortex is employed by the universe as a whole in the manifestation of its elementary forms. Vortex theory took second place to the nascent atomic theory of nineteenth-century physics, but quantum theory is now realizing that the "elementary particles" of the universe are not in fact solids, but are formed by spinning—and thus inherently stable—"strings" or vortices of energy that, unlike matter, can cross and exist in many dimensions. Such vortices apparently have edges, but their energy extends outward in subtle fields (such as Sheldrake's "morphenogenetic" fields) that fill and are in fact responsible for space. The apparent "edges" of forms are merely subjective impressions created by the interaction between them and the observer sharing a dimensional field.

Spiritual thinkers have long held the universe is resonant, multidimensional and interdependent. Healers have long worked with the vortical energies of the chakras through which the soul or light body manifests. Sir George Trevelyan encouraged opening the vortex of the crown chakra "to bring the Christ energy down to earth."

The Vortical Waters of Avalon

From an esoteric point of view the human body, our 'mortal coil,' is informed by an energy vortex, an 'immortal coil,' that through a set of spinning chakras forms the vehicle for the soul's passage through the sublunary sphere. The Egyptians called this energy or light body the *ka*. The individual *psyche*, soul, is energy on a journey of incoming and outgoing through the *anima mundi*, the collective world soul. The body—which is mostly water—takes its vortical shape around the incoming force of the energy body, and loses its shape as its energy fields return, at death, to other dimensions.

The vortex is the pattern preferred by water and by all structures in water-dependent biological worlds. The vortex is present everywhere, including the genetic encoding of the 'double helix' of DNA. The multiple layering of a vortex allows the greatest interaction between the elements within it. The dissolving upon stirring of sugar or salt crystals in a glass of water provides a perfect illustration of the effectiveness of this sort of interaction. An essential procedure of the alchemists was the *solutio*, in which the contents of the retort could be dissolved back into the *prima materia* as a first step in purification, preliminary to the creation of a new form. In this process, the mysterious *Mercurius* acted both as the 'supreme solvent' and as the base matter to which the alchemist must return before making further progress.

While the Tor functions as an alchemical retort or alembic, its alchemical potency is due to the fact it is also a point of interaction and connection with the revolving heavenly dimension. In northern Europe, the summit of the *axis mundi*, the World Mountain, is attached to the Pole Star around which revolve the heavens—sometimes shown as the twelve houses of the Zodiac. The *axis mundi* is the conductor of celestial energy, sometimes shown as lightning from the Gods and thus the passageway between the worlds. In the Celtic tradition, the Tor as a revolving and brilliant spiral castle—*Caer Sidi*—also receives and steps down the energies of the greater cosmos. At the same time, the water and the iron in the aquifer that forms its core may increase the Tor's receptivity to fields of celestial energy, such as the magnetic and electromagnetic fields of the sun.

The Tor viewed from the North

The sun has a constant, if changing, influence upon the electromagnetic fields, atmosphere, elements, water and the iron core of the earth. The ionic charge of the simple hydrogen atom, so prevalent in water, in our bodies and throughout the cosmos (it forms over seventy percent of all its measurable mass) becomes highly active under solar influence. Water develops its highest levels of ionisation while in a rapidly moving vortex like a mountain stream exposed to the sun, and can even generate a detectable electrical charge when moving slowly through the threadlike veins of a typical subterranean aquifer.

With high ionisation, the molecules of water become loosely bonded together and the vortices that form their electrons are in a state of flux. Water is able to maintain its purity, develop and enhance life through its ability to receive, dissolve, transform and transmit the nature of other substances and their electromagnetic charges as it encounters them within a vortex. Through the calcium and iron in the upper and lower parts of its aquifer, together with the solvent and vortical effects of water, Glastonbury Tor maintains a specific energetic polarity that makes it highly receptive to subtle celestial influences.

The matter that forms the brain should be understood esoterically as a receiver of the energy of consciousness, not, as is presently thought, the generator of it. The 'alchemisation' or release of spirit from the soul means the opening of the windows of perception to those energetic spheres beyond the four dimensions of the sublunary realm. The alchemists knew that the vortex-like energies of *Mercurius* as the supreme solvent and the medium *par excellence* of matter's receptivity regulated processes of physical embodiment and also allowed consciousness to be purified.

In its transformational journey between the spheres, the soul is greatly affected by the quality of the vibrational forces or energy fields around it. At one level, these fields can be imagined as forming quite raw energies that could engross the soul in dense matter—these are the most elemental, *daemonic* forces of the sublunary *anima mundi*. Some alchemists under Christian and Gnostic influence fell into a position of dualism—where matter is seen as evil. But core alchemical tradition saw material forces as creating a 'seed bed' for more refined energies. They saw this ambivalent energy as *Mercurius*.

In the Glastonbury tradition, the alchemists' "heavenly dew" is shown on the coat of arms of St. Joseph of Arimathea alongside the two cruets containing water and blood. This dew precipitated the conditions for the complete reunion of opposites that led to the Philosophers' Stone. Through this process, the alchemists tried to manifest simultaneously fully incarnate yet completely spiritual forms. The same goal is shared by Christianity in the transubstantiation of the white and red substances of the Eucharist. Alchemy held that spirit's immanence in the world could be made manifest through their processes of transmutation, revealed in the gold of the philosopher's stone. In the alchemical mysteries of Avalon the surrounding energetic fields, combined with the vortical power of water, catalyse similar processes in the individual soul.

The coat of arms of Joseph of Arimathea, showing the two cruets, a cross made from the Holy Thorn and drops of 'Heavenly Dew'.

King Arthur's Court

In the same way as water is supported through its flow in vortex forms to create optimum conditions for the development of life, we can see how the soul can be supported and transmuted through a sympathetic vortical medium. The resonance between the receptive and energetic qualities of water and the supramental capacity of 'mind' facilitates an energy vortex appropriate for the meeting of subtle energies—and consequently for soul transition, growth and transformation. Those people in the past who sensed the ability of the subtle energy fields of the water in the Tor to respond to focused intention would have gathered on the Isle of Avalon to conduct practices that supported these purposes.

One place they would have gathered was at the meeting place of the two springs, at what is now King Arthur's Court in the centre of Chalice Well Gardens (where Miller and Broadhurst report the Michael and Mary lines intersect). This was the focus of healing activity in the mid eighteenth-century and the outline of the baths and the bathhouse are still there in the flagstones today. As the original meeting place of the two springs at the heart of what is now Chalice Well, the Court reproduces on a small and accessible scale the vortical energies of the aquifer contained within the Tor.

Dion Fortune in her garden near the White Spring.

The Alchemy of Avalon

That two springs, one red and one white, should rise together and flow out from one of the most remarkable hills in the British Isles strikes a profound chord in the imagination. In esoteric tradition, the Tor as world centre and *axis mundi* provides the means of passage between the mundane world and the spiritual realms. In such a place, the veils separating ordinary reality from spiritual planes can thin or dissolve, allowing those who are receptive to receive the guidance and blessings of the otherworld. The guardian spirits of the Avalonian soul-portal invite all those who are drawn here to pass through the symbolic gateway that is the Tor. The interplay between the subtle energies of the Red and White Springs is a vital key to understanding the impact of this experience upon the individual soul-body.

Mercurius, the divine hermaphrodite, both sun and moon, red and white, stands in the centre of the mandorla. Turba philosophorum, *Ms. Lat. 7171, Bibliothèque de l'Arsenal, Paris, sixteenth century, f.16.*

The springs of Avalon have very powerful effects upon those who visit them, both to drink their waters and also, as attested over the centuries by many visitors, to attune to the subtle transformative energies of their guardian spirits. These revitalising waters aid in the stepping down and balanced assimilation of the intense spiritual forces focused upon the Tor. Through contact with the gentler healing powers of the two springs, the seeker can become aligned with the hidden energies of the Tor, where, in a manner equivalent to the transformation taking place in an alchemical alembic, they can receive initiation.

The Avalonian soul-portal can be envisioned as the distinctive oval shape that forms the centre of the *vesica piscis* design on the lid of the Red Spring's wellhead. This almond shape is a *mandorla*, a symbol of rebirth and spiritual regeneration. Its shape also corresponds to the *yoni*, the female genitals, and to an ancient part of the brain influencing emotional responses and emotional memory, the *amygdala*—meaning 'almond shaped.' The effect of such esoteric seed-symbols upon our etheric bodies is vastly accelerated when the symbols are manifested in sacred sites that function as energy vortices and planetary portals. For those who are receptive to such sites, they stimulate an intense and ongoing process of personal transformation, in which the soul, the *ka,* or light body, is slowly 'alchemised'—purified and finally transmuted—through infusion with the 'golden' radiance of spirit. As it bathes in a grail-like stream of compassionate wisdom that comes through the portal, and is both solar and stellar in origin, the individual light-body is slowly cleansed of accumulated negativity and trauma. This process unfolds over the course of successive visits, infusing the soul more and more thoroughly with healing energies. When the work of alchemisation is complete, the light-body is able to assist in the work of the fifth dimension, the realm of the guardian spirits and the higher planetary guides. But this work is often slow and painful, and is sometimes blocked for long periods.

Red & White Symbolism in Esoteric Teachings

The symbolism of red and white springs or fountains has an exact parallel in medieval and Renaissance European alchemy. Red and white (sometimes gold and white) colours and fluids also have an important place in other occult traditions, especially those of India, Egypt and Tibet. Understood in these teachings as the two great creative and opposing principles upon which planetary existence is founded, the controlled interplay of red and white forces is used to map initiatory journeys of spiritual purification. These patterns are encoded in transformative, chemical, biochemical, geophysical and psycho-spiritual processes.

The red and white substances are imaged as fire and water, sun and moon, blood and milk (or white sexual fluids), and often as masculine and feminine, king and queen, or god and goddess. Yet the attributes of the two principles may be differently assigned. In Western alchemy, for example, the feminine principle is white, the masculine red, while in Hindu and Buddhist Tantra the polarity is usually reversed: the Tantric goddess Kundalini Shakti is red in colour, and her consort the god Shiva is a brilliant white. The red and white principles may also be of the same gender: the tutelary goddesses of Upper and Lower Egypt were the red cobra goddess Udjit and the white vulture goddess Nekhebet. Their union was imaged in the double, red and white, crown of the Pharaoh.

Through the interplay, refinement and eventual 'marriage' of these opposing principles in the body and soul of the initiate, the divine spark in matter and the soul is realised and slowly transmuted. Finally, it manifests a product given many different names: the Philosophers' Stone that can transmute base matter to gold; the Vedic *soma,* or elixir of immortality; the radiant, wish-fulfilling jewel of the Tibetan *cintamani,* or the enlightened, 'adamantine' mind.

Before we describe alchemy, let us emphasise that the alchemy of Avalon involves a complex process of initiation, in which both collective human consciousness and the planetary light or life-body are raised to higher frequencies. If enough people move into this state, and are willing to accept the responsibility that comes with heightened responsiveness to elemental, planctary, transplanetary and spiritual energies, these forces can help to transform the grave ecological and cultural crisis of our planet into an opportunity—an accelerated process of rebalancing and healing whose aim is planetary service. By hastening the release of human consciousness from identification with dualism, and by learning to transmit radiant streams of the elixir-like energy of love-wisdom from the portal opened by the *opus*, the alchemised soul learns to connect with and honour all beings.

European Alchemy: "Make one water out of the two waters" (Trimosin, *Splendor Solis*)

Western alchemy is a slippery subject. It uses enigmas, paradoxes and half-broken codes to remind us that the mind alone cannot understand its esoteric aims—instead, we need to connect alchemical symbols with experiential knowledge. Below is a brief outline of alchemy's central concepts.

The alchemical process begins with the creation of an elusive substance called the *prima materia* or 'first matter.' This substance is 'our mercury' or *Mercurius*, which is the catalyst of the entire work. A symbolic descent into the cavernous depths of the earth is the essential starting point of the work, for at the spiritual level, alchemy requires the initiatory journey to begin with a visit to the underworld. The sixteenth-century English alchemist Philalethes wrote that the seeker must "descend /Into himself the matter for to finde/ Of this our stone." This preliminary descent into the chaos of matter is called the *nigredo*—the blackening.

The Mercurial worms in the nigredo, represented by a raven's head, begin the work of transforming the base matter. Anatomiae auri sive tyrocinium medico-chymicum, *J. D. Mylius, Frankfort, 1628.*

Mercurius is an ambivalent yet fundamentally transformative force, equivalent to the spirit hidden in matter. Change and circularity is the essence of this trickster-like principle, indeed it is dual-natured or hermaphroditic. As the base metal put in the alembic is reduced to a primal formlessness, Mercurius's first appearance is as a fierce dragon or serpent that begins the work by devouring his own tail. Mercurial 'worms' or serpents are often depicted in the alembic at the first stage of the work to represent matter feeding upon itself, but it is essential to understand that these mercurial serpents are also the means of matter's regeneration. Through the effects of Mercurius, the *prima materia* is separated into two opposing principles, a red substance and a white substance, and through Mercurius again, these white and red substances are repeatedly separated and reunited, in a process called *solve et coagula*.

Frequently represented as two separated springs or fountains, the red and white substances have contrasting chemical functions: the red is associated with heat and congeals or fixes a form; the white, identified with cold and wateriness, dissolves form. The two substances repeatedly combine and separate in several distinct chemical stages, each of which includes a *coniunctio* or 'chemical wedding' and a dissolution or 'death.' At crucial stages in the process, the physical substance corresponding to the soul or light-body is progressively transmuted and 'dyed' through a complete spectrum of colours, from black to violet or crimson red. In the final stages of the work, when the interaction of these two substances is highly refined, two elixirs are produced; firstly, a white elixir, and subsequently a red elixir. These represent the two fundamental parts of the final elixir that is the king and queen's androgynous child: the *lapis philosophorum*, the Philosophers' Stone, the stone of the wise. This is depicted in many ways, but sometimes as a star-surrounded hill or mount, a tree, or as an overflowing cup or grail.

Mercurius, here depicted as a woman holding a dragon, stands upon the red and white fountains that represent the alchemical work. Thomas Aquinas (pseud.), De alchimia, *MS. Paris, sixteenth century.*

The white stream, often described as silver (as a distinct aspect of 'our mercury'), is the focus of a watery process of dissolution or cleansing called the *albedo*—the whitening. This phase follows the *nigredo*, in a repeated breaking down of form or matter that purifies it, preparing soul to receive illumination from spirit. Mercurial waters now cleanse the substance, by rising as a vapour in the alembic and descending again as revivifying 'dew.' The feminine principle, *Luna*, or the White Queen, is dominant in this stage of whitening, which finally produces a white powder, stone or elixir.

The final stage of the work, called the *rubedo*—the reddening—is ruled over by Sol, or the Red King. It is a stage connected with fire, and hence with the power of the sun. Now the red substance imposes form on the formlessness of the white stone through a process of heating, sometimes described as a congealing process, that turns the white to a red powder. This is intended to be a permanent change of colour representing the embodiment or 'fixation' of spirit, but like every stage of alchemy, it may have to be repeated many times. Because the red proceeds from the white stage, it is often said that within the whiteness the red is hidden. Alchemist Benjamin Lock wrote: "The first part of the Elixir is made of white earth, and therefore is white. The second part is red for it is made of red earth, yet nevertheless it is one Elixir and no more." The final alchemical synthesis of the red and white thus produces an understanding akin to the Buddhist aphorism: "Form is Emptiness, and Emptiness is Form."

The distinctive colour of sky blue or azure is often associated with the final achievement of the alchemical stone or tincture that can transmute to gold. Seventeenth-century alchemist Thomas Vaughan described the stone as "a certain inexpressible Azure like the Body of Heaven in a clear Day." In Egyptian alchemy, the transforming substance was represented by a pale blue lotus. In medieval alchemy, blue-azure is the colour of Mercurius, as the spirit released from matter that becomes the agent of matter's final spiritualisation. The importance of this colour can be compared to the experience of 'Ground Luminosity,' the infinite space or Clear Light of the Void that is fundamental to the enlightenment-mind of Tibetan Buddhism.

Eastern Alchemies: *Soma* in the *Rig Veda* & *Bodhicitta* in the Tibetan Tradition

The *Rig Veda*, oldest of the Indian Vedic texts, tells how a miraculous substance called *soma* was used in secret rituals that led to immortality and the extension of the subtle body of light. Soma means 'to extract or press out' and was identified with several plant substances. It was described as the union of fire and water, sun and moon, heaven and earth. Understood as the fundamental energy source of all other energies, including matter itself, soma was reputed not only to bestow bliss and wisdom, but also to give long life, even immortality. At a crucial stage in the soma ceremony a white soma was generated—possibly through extraction from a plant called *haoma*—then mixed with another, solar, liquid, to prepare an elixir of immortality, sometimes called *amrita*. This was the 'golden soma,' seen as a golden fountain or pillar of light manifesting, through ritual, in a sacred place identified with the *axis mundi* and representing the creative energy of the universe. The white soma was the means of uniting the priest to this golden column. There is a correspondence to this outward process within the physical body, where the priest taking part in the soma ceremony is bathed in a descending dew of heavenly white soma. This gathers in the heart, and generates an immortal, golden, spirit-body, extending heavenwards like a pillar and associated with fire and the sun.

Central to both Tibetan and Hindu Tantra is a mystic union of opposites that enables the initiate to move out of a dualistic ego-centered experience and enter a unitary field of perception in which s/he is no longer separate, but part of a cosmic web of energies where everything is irradiated by the purest light. Whether or not sexual congress is explicitly part of Tantric practice, the need to transcend the polarity of masculine and feminine principles is emphasised by images of deities in sexual union. These entwined figures represent the union of compassion (*upaya*) and wisdom (*prajna*) that is the actuality of enlightenment. Some tantric teachings maintain that only the tantric path to enlightenment can be fully efficacious in the *Kali Yuga*—our current age of materialism and chaos.

In Tantra, the focus is on directing red and white energies, the red and white *bodhicitta*, through the central column and medial nerve of the spine. *Bodhicitta* means 'enlightenment-mind.' Red *bodhicitta* is identified with the female sexual essence and represents the seed of wisdom; white *bodhicitta* is the male sexual essence and represents the seed of compassion. The two currents of *bodhicitta* are purified through meditation, using a force called the 'inner mystic heat.' The desired result is that the red *bodhicitta*, equated with kundalini energy and the rising flame of spiritual awareness, rises from the root chakra to the crown chakra, where its fiery heat releases the purified white nectar, the creative principle or 'elixir of enlightenment-consciousness.' This descends throughout the body, clearing karma and creating a state of ecstatic joy, while in the heart centre the red and white *bodhicittas* are united as clear light and awareness of emptiness, or the all-embracing love of the enlightened mind.

In Tibetan 'Pure Land' teachings and in other Eastern traditions that trace their origins back to the *Vedas*, there are further descriptions of red as well as white 'essences.' "During the development of the fetus," Sogyal Rinpoche writes in *The Tibetan Book of Living and Dying*, "our father's essence, a nucleus that is... 'white and blissful,' rests in the chakra at the crown of our head at the top of the central channel. The mother's essence, a nucleus that is 'red and hot,' rests in the chakra... below the navel." At the end of life, the teachings say, the white essence descends the central channel of the body; as it approaches the heart, it induces an experience of "whiteness." Thereafter, the corresponding ascent of the mother's essence induces an experience of "redness." When the essences are united and balanced in the heart, Tibetan Buddhists say that the mind is at last free of thoughts and there dawns "the mind of clear light."

It seems therefore that Vedic, Hindu and Buddhist traditions concerning the esoteric symbolism of red and white share many similarities with the Western equivalent of Tantra, alchemy.

The Isle of Glass as Alchemical 'Glass'

The primary ingredients of the alchemical *opus* are alternately heated and cooled within a sealed container of some kind. This container is the alchemical vessel or alembic, yet it is also the human body, as in Tantra. In geomantic terms, the alembic is a sacred landscape, a world pillar or *axis mundi,* where the world-spirit, the *spiritus mundi*, is highly concentrated. Alchemists called the alembic the 'glass-house' or 'glass,' and on the greater geomantic scale, the symbolism evokes Avalon as the legendary 'Ynys Witrin' or the Isle of Glass. Avalon functions as the alembic for all who visit the island as pilgrims.

Like the seven-tiered labyrinth around the Tor, the alchemical process is often described as sevenfold. But there are three key stages, corresponding to the colours black, white and red. These different phases of the Work phases of the Work correspond to the spiritual effects of the landscape around the Tor:

1. The *nigredo* or black phase. The alchemical process begins with a symbolic death—a painful descent into the underworld-like chaos of unformed matter. This corresponds to some major crisis—a frustration of goals or desires, leading to a loss of life-direction and accompanying depression—that prompts a change of life-path and spiritual reorientation. In the geomancy of Avalon, the underworld associated with the Tor, its fairy kingdom and its hidden caverns corresponds closely to this process. Through journeying to the Tor, symbolic entry is achieved to the underworld of Avalon, ruled over by the Fairy King and Queen, Gwynn ap Nudd and Morgan le Fay. Those beginning the initiatory journey are figuratively sealed within the Avalonian alembic. A return to this painful and purgative phase may be repeated several times and can be associated with what is locally called the 'Glastonbury Experience.'

2. The *albedo* or white phase. This second stage, also repeated many times, is ruled by the feminine principle as a white goddess or queen figure, Luna. This is a process of washing or purification through water called the *solutio* or dissolution. Its purpose is to begin the release of the spirit, or of a new life cleansed of the past. At this stage, the body's experience of a loss of form is repeated, but now with more blissful accompanying states. These may be triggered by erotic love, by the use of psychoactive substances, or by an intense experience of healing and mystic union.

This phase of indistinctness, of waiting for a new identity to be formed, can be associated specifically with the White Spring, and more generally with the protection of the Goddess. It also relates to a geophysical and mystical phenomenon sometimes called the 'White Lady' or the 'Mists of Avalon.' Through a growing understanding of these energies, initiates are taken under the healing mantle of the Goddess in one of her many forms, such as Brighde, Isis or Mary, and begin to see through and disperse the astral mists of illusion, attachment to bliss states and spiritual glamour that are initially encountered by the seeker. During the *albedo*, the initiate begins to work with inner and outer polarities, and may enter into one or more 'chemical weddings,' perhaps represented by different relationships or by a single, evolving relationship. However, the frequent psychic disturbances in the environment of Avalon suggest that this stage is not easy for the Avalonian initiate to complete; a balance between emotion and intellect is required for the transition to the final phase of the *rubedo*. It is very important that the phenomena connected with this phase of 'whitening' are not confused with the successful completion of the 'Great Work.'

3. The *rubedo* or red phase. Closely linked with the Red Spring, this phase is informed by different kinds of fire and light—especially by the solar rays, meteorological and electromagnetic energies concentrated at different times of the year around the Tor. The energies of the Red Spring are particularly strong at key moments in the pre-Christian calendar: at the old fire festivals of Imbolc, Beltane, Lammas and Samhain, and at the Equinoxes and Solstices that mark changes in the sun's passage in relation to the earth. In the last century, the spiritual powers of the Red Spring were cultivated and focused by Wellesley Tudor Pole, a man overshadowed by the Archangel Michael. Sir George Trevelyan frequently described the gold-white energies of the Christ descending through the crown chakra to meet the red energies of the base chakra. This infusion represented the sacralising of the Earth; and certainly the Chalice Well garden is infused with high levels of the solar pranic currents connected with both St. Michael and the Christ. Michael's sword is represented in both the house and gardens; his spear, also connected with the wounding of Christ, is shown on the lid of the wellhead. At the Lion's head and Arthur's Court there are hints of the link between the Red Spring's healing power and a solar energy connected with mythic kingship. The Grail mythos links that power with the themes of both masculine sacrifice and feminine offering.

The deepest spiritual energies of the Red Spring relate to the future: to the emergence of a reborn and rebalanced divine masculine energy that can complement and eventually conjoin with the Goddess energy that is so venerated in Avalon. This last stage of the alchemical work, involving the balanced union of a rejuvenated solar king-god with a goddess-queen in a symbolic heart centre, such as the pool in King Arthur's Court, has long been delayed by our neglect of the divine feminine.

Since the recent cleansing of the White Spring, the spiritual and healing powers of the two springs can now manifest in a more balanced way, as can the different phases of the Avalonian alchemy. Visitors to both springs have reported sightings of a transparent white lady, while increasing numbers now see or sense an earthy masculine presence connected with Gwynn, Lord of the Tor. At the Red Spring's wellhead, visitors may sense a pale blue column of light that evokes the androgynous Mercurius, alchemical catalyst and world-spirit, as it moves up and down the pillar-like energy of the axis mundi. Elsewhere in Chalice Well garden and in the adjoining house of Little St. Michael's, there have been visions of healing beings identified with

St. Michael or the Christ energy.

In the psycho-spiritual terms of the western Hermetic tradition, the achievement of the Stone or elixir involves a miraculous commingling of spirit and matter—a full rebirth of the human as a 'royal' being with an imperishable 'body of light.' To achieve this final blissful integration of opposites requires a departure from all that has gone before. Often described as a 'leap' of consciousness, it is the leap beyond polarity in which the initiate abandons the entire conceptual framework through which s/he has formerly viewed reality. The identification and objectification of matter that comes from the over-valuation of the intellect falls away, to be replaced by a balance between subject and object, mind and matter, this world and the next. All that supports the ego is stripped away in the vessel of purification, and the light of the divine takes its place.

The reborn one may be described as an immortal, an *akh* or 'shining one' in Egyptian lore, an *augeoides* or luminous 'star-body' in Greek Neoplatonism, a *vajra*-being who has achieved a pristine or 'diamond-like' consciousness in Vajrayana Buddhism, or as an ascended one possessed of an inner 'sun-chariot' or *merkabah* in Kabbalistic lore and recent New Age teachings. The shining one recovers a pre-conceptual state beyond the conflicts created by duality, becoming at one with a pure realm associated with the sun and stars, but crucially also enjoying a new state of harmony with nature. As the perfect inherent form of everything is perceived by this rebalanced consciousness, the new shining one is released from the confining mind-set and death-bound course of linear time into the cyclic flow of cosmic life itself.

The Matter of Britain

The Avalonian alchemy does not only act strongly upon the individual visitor; it has also imprinted and continually transmuted the group-soul of the island nation of Britain, of which the Isle of Avalon is the esoteric microcosm and *nemeton*, or sanctuary. Indeed, Britain's guardianship of powerful alchemical mysteries may explain the frequent description of the British Isles as an earthly paradise by the ancients who first travelled here. In its myths and landscape, Avalon is closely associated with the esoteric material known as the 'Matter of Britain.' The term refers to the corpus of myth, legend, history and symbolism that provides the British with vital insights into their origins, the nature of British sovereignty, the unfolding destiny of the nation and their relationship to the rest of the world. It also represents a native spiritual tradition of initiation by which both the individual and the group-soul can come to realise their true nature.

In the Avalonian tradition, the exemplary royal couple, Arthur and Guinevere, were reputed to have been buried in the Abbey grounds. Excalibur was said to have been made at Avalon and returned to the waters there at Pomparles Bridge ('Perilous Bridge' at the tip of Wearyall Hill). A local legend tells that the Grail itself is buried below Chalice Hill. But to identify the alchemical character of British sovereignty and its links to Avalon we need to consider a striking theme that repeats itself in the ancient literature; this concerns two dragons, one red and one white. In Geoffrey of Monmouth's *History of the Kings of Britain* Vortigern, pretender to the throne of Britain, is persuaded by his magicians to build a stronghold after his collusion in a massacre of British leaders. The episode occurred in the period of turmoil after the Roman withdrawal, when the Saxons were invading from the east and the issue of British sovereignty—dormant for so long—had been reopened. Vortigern was foiled in his attempt to obtain sovereignty, because two white and red dragons were fighting below the foundations of his castle. This was revealed to him by the magician Merlin, who also prophesied his death.

In an earlier text, the Welsh *Mabinogion,* a similar picture is drawn when three plagues ravage the land during the reign of King Lludd. No solution is found until Lludd is told by his brother Llevelys to overcome two struggling dragons and bury them "within the strongest place you know of in the island," which happened to be near Oxford. These are seemingly the same two dragons who appear later under Vortigern's castle. At stake in both stories is the sovereignty and health of the land; the dragons shake down Vortigern's castle because he is unfit to be king. These dragons or serpents represent the polarised forces of the sublunary realm, from which we may understand that their balance produces initiation into true sovereignty—true planetary or world service.

It is said that at the time of Uther Pendragon, the father of Arthur, the standard of Britain was a red dragon and a white dragon. Pendragon means the 'head of the dragon' and the figure of the dragon in this epoch signified wisdom and courage. As a result of a vision received by Arthur (at Beckery, just west of Glastonbury) in which Mary and the Christ child appeared, Arthur put away the old standard and created a new one based upon a cross, three crowns and the Holy Mother and Child. Shortly after this Arthur was defeated at Camlann and retired to Avalon to heal his wounds. The old standard was divided, with the white dragon going to the Saxons in the east and the red dragon going to the Welsh (the Celts or the original Britons) in the west.

The theme of conflict and union between two forces or sides holding a red or a white symbol has reappeared several times in English and British myth and history. Around 1277, England adopted the red and white cross of St. George as its national flag, but in the late medieval Wars of the Roses the red-white polarity resurfaced in the conflict between the Houses of Lancaster and York. The victor in that war, Henry VII, sought to heal the ancient symbolic division of Britain reopened in the Wars of the Roses. Henry understood the power present in symbols; he fought under a standard of the red dragon, claimed descent from King Arthur (through Offa and Cadwallader), and named his first son Arthur. On his accession, he used his marriage to a white queen—Elizabeth of York—to claim a quasi-alchemical image of royal power: the red and white Tudor rose. British monarchs have claimed sovereignty ever since through the line of descent and the symbols Henry established. Today, the red lion and the white unicorn support the British royal arms.

The Coat of Arms of the present Prince of Wales.

Alchemy explains the striking prominence of a red and white polarity in the mythology and symbolism of British sovereignty. The alchemical work is carried out through the successive union and separation of opposites until the final *coniunctio* or the 'Royal Marriage' can take place. In the context of the Matter of Britain, the Philosophers' Stone represents the purified and balanced 'sovereignty' produced by the Royal Marriage—and from this stone comes the sword of truth and justice. This is the union of a 'true' King and Queen: that is, of two enlightened beings who embody the polarity of the world spirit and the unity of spirit both within and between themselves. In the context of Avalon, we may imagine the royal couple bathing in the joint stream of energy created by the merging of the Red and White Springs. We may imagine the queen-goddess marrying the king-god in the crucible of the holy well, symbolising the blessing of the Holy Grail, and the manifestation of the divine qualities of truth, justice, order, inspiration, healing and abundance throughout the land.

The Royal Couple having achieved the coniunctio *through all the stages of the work—represented by seven steps or tiers—sit in a sumptuous pavilion within a water-surrounded mount. The Phoenix of Spirit rises from the roof and the Zodiac turns about the whole. Figures representing the planets stand on the terraces of the mount, while the fountain of Mercurius crowns the summit. A blindfolded man represents the human condition, that is, until he is willing to enter the cave. Steffan Michelspacher,* Cabala, speculum artis et naturae, in alchymia*, Augsburg, 1654, plate 3.*

Conclusion

The Red and the White Springs of Avalon represent all the polarities that shape the entire sublunary sphere. Alchemy, as the western form of Tantra, hints that the *mandorla* or *vesica piscis* represents the gateway towards the unification or balance between these polarities, thereby enabling the soul to enter into a transfigured cosmos. To grasp this subtle concept means grasping the nature of *Mercurius*, the alchemical solvent that is neither of this world or the next, but can teach the initiate the sacred relationship between 'base' matter and the divine. It is not that the external world is transcended through initiation, nor that the internal world is all there is. Instead, alchemy teaches that the inner and the outer worlds—self and the other, soul and the world, soul and spirit—can finally meet and confirm each other in the experience of the fully awakened individual.

Viewed in this way, the waters of the White Spring, emerging from the calciferous caverns under the Tor, balanced with the rubeate waters of its partner Chalice Well, establish in the Avalonian landscape a physical expression of the unified inner order not just of the self, but of Britain, the sacred world and the realm of the divine. Rising from their mysterious subterranean source in the *axis mundi*, the two springs are more than a mere physical or even symbolic representation of truths found in the inner world. They uphold the 'gold' of resolved or unified matter; they refine and release the individual spirit body, while also maintaining the nature, health and harmony of the land of Britain. When seen as a physical manifestation of the earth-spirit, not just its symbol, both the springs of Avalon and the *axis mundi* from which they flow attest to the transformative spiritual powers that are miraculously hidden in the interior of the earth.

When its mysterious powers are recognised by the soul on the quest for spirit, Avalon offers an initiatory journey—a Mercurial voyage between the within and the without—that cannot be achieved through subjective, inner practice alone. Through engagement with the Avalonian gateway of the *mandorla*, an objective geomantic alchemy is initiated, in which the soul, through the refinement of increasingly purified elixirs or essences, may achieve at-onement with the Universal Mind. In the process, different kinds of Royal Marriage, "chymical weddings" of varying colours or 'shades,' will be experienced: within soul's own nature; with the *anima mundi*, the world soul; with other souls on the same journey; and finally with spirit.

The Glastonbury Experience & the Path of Initiation

What is called the 'Glastonbury Experience' can be understood as a distinctive and often highly intense aspect of the initiatory journey of the soul that corresponds closely to the alchemical *nigredo*. Profound and frequently painful forms of initiatory experience are undergone by all who strive to move forward on the spiritual path, although the particular character and timing of an initiation, or new stage of soul awakening, is always unique to each individual. As the seeker gradually comes to understand their individual soul-nature and starts to address the inner obstacles to true soul-growth, they are confronted at different stages on their journey by specific barriers: some of these will be created by the personality or ego, others by culture and society, other by ancient traumas or imbalances that are part of the individual soul-memory (or karma). In the case of the 'Glastonbury experience', however, this initiatory journey becomes curiously place-specific. All of those who connect with the place as Avalon—that is, who travel here as pilgrims—are making a choice at the soul level, although sometimes without conscious awareness of this, to submit to a profound and potentially ongoing version of the process of initiation.[1] For those who actually move to live in Glastonbury, this process can become especially intense.

The Path of Initiation

Although its outer forms may sometimes appear to be different, the initiatory process has common features in all religious and spiritual traditions. In Buddhist tradition, the journey of the Buddha towards enlightenment combines worldly renunciation and austerity with the use of meditative techniques to quiet the overactive mind, cultivating detachment and inner peace; significantly, the Buddha's inner journey is also connected with a profound reconnection with the natural world. He leaves the city and enters the forest, where he teaches the deer and finally finds enlightenment under a bodhi tree, assisted by a serpent deity called the Naga King as well as by the Earth Mother. In Christian tradition, the equivalent initiatory path is represented most clearly by the discipline and unworldliness of the monastic life, which began in the early Christian era with monks moving to live in the desert between Egypt and Palestine. Christian mystical tradition sees a 'dark night of the soul' as central to the process of inner purification, and often compares the soul's initiatory journey to stages in the life of Jesus Christ, culminating in his crucifixion and resurrection. Here, as in several other mystical traditions, including forms of Hindu asceticism and Buddhist tantra, the individual's meditation upon suffering, death and the impermanence of the flesh is a vital stage in the initiatory process.

In Celtic myth and in the Grail legends that it shaped, a commitment to the initiatory journey is often represented by the crossing of one or more 'perilous bridges'. These dangerous crossings are the testing gateways to the Grail Castle, where deeper spiritual insights may be obtained. These bridges are extremely narrow and dangerous, often made of glass or swords or even of water. They present the seeker who approaches them with a decisive choice—to leave ordinary reality and its rational rules behind and enter into an otherworldly dimension that is governed by strict spiritual laws. When you approach the Isle of Avalon from the south-west today, along the causewayed road that leads from the town of Street, you still cross onto the island over a bridge across the River Brue. The monks of Glastonbury called this Pomparles Bridge, 'pont perilous', and they associated it with a critical point in Arthurian legend, as the place where Sir Bedivere returns Arthur's sword Excalibur to its primary guardian, the Lady of the Lake. In esoteric terms, any spiritually-motivated journey to Glastonbury can be understood as an invitation to cross over a perilous bridge—to traverse the gulf or 'abyss' that separates our first stages of inner awakening from states of higher consciousness.[2] Moving to live here, however, imposes a more urgent and unavoidable pressure, for the appeal of the inner guardians of the island is that the seeker now begins to live a new kind of life, one of spiritual service. Whether this choice is made consciously or not, the new resident is now subject to the mysterious rules that operate in otherworldly realms—often with alarming and painful effects on their individual lives.

The Chalice Well.

However one sees the Avalonian challenge, to rise to it fully appears always to require a commitment to some form of spiritual service, and also a submission to an inner discipline not unlike that of the long-dead monks of the 'Company of Avalon', who communicated with Frederick Bligh Bond at the turn of the 20th century. An individual who embarks on a permanent crossing into Avalon is being asked, not to become wholly unworldly or impractical, but certainly to begin to change their attitude to all that defines mundane reality, or 'the world'. This inner journey of purification commences with the pilgrim's first arrival, but it will normally unfold over many years, through successive personal experiences of the *nigredo*. Each seeker will be tested in different ways, as they encounter and try to come to terms with manifold aspects of their 'shadow' selves.

In any initiatory process, such as those offered by the ancient mystery schools and all authentic spiritual traditions, the aim is to break down the shells or barriers that form the ego and outer personality, and awaken the indwelling soul. This process of soul cleansing and rebalancing, sometimes called the 'Great Work,' is one of moving from being centered (and often engulfed) in a 'self' engendered by temporal and social circumstances into the 'true self,' the eternal soul. The work typically happens in stages, via different kinds of crisis, each potentially followed by illumination. The crises—emotional, psychological, financial, physical, professional and spiritual—are directly or indirectly triggered by the individual seeker's request or perhaps unconscious wish for the next level of initiation. This inner work is extremely hard and challenging; because of this—especially when society offers only an ego- and materially-identified existence—the awakening soul may choose to go back to sleep and postpone the spiritual work until a later incarnation. Yet when an awakening soul comes to a spiritual centre such as Glastonbury, the work of soul-purging can either spontaneously begin or is accelerated, whether it is consciously sought for or not. This process can feel unrelenting and, at times, unbearable.

The Alchemical Island

Glastonbury's ancient name of *Ynis Witrin*, the Isle of Glass, reminds us that this glass house, castle or island functions as an alchemical alembic or container. Entering Glastonbury or the Isle of Glass with the intention to stay commits one to undergoing an individual process of soul-alchemy, as one becomes sealed in the container that is the island and the fire or light of spirit is applied to its contents. At some level, but to different degrees, because each soul that moves to Avalon has made a conscious or unconscious choice to accelerate the processing of their individual karma, they will at some point meet the dark shadows that are thrown up by the unfolding inner light. As successive illusions and attachments are burnt away in the fire applied to the alembic, we can feel desolate indeed. When one is in the midst of a

Glastonbury experience, the inner guardians of this place can appear as terrible and merciless, like Buddhist or Hindu wrathful deities; ultimately, however, they are functioning as compassionate local midwives, assisting us in a profound process of soul rebirth. For their aim in triggering any intense experience of suffering is to move the individual soul into a purer state of consciousness and way of living—and into a more effective and heart-felt life of spiritual service.

The timing and duration of this process varies considerably. It may begin soon after moving to Glastonbury or may not be initiated until many years after arrival. It may proceed as a series of crisis-waves spaced over several years, each alchemical *nigredo* or 'blackening' making a further contribution to the life-long work of breaking down those barriers that prevent the soul from attuning to higher spiritual teachings. The Glastonbury experience can sometimes be a 'dark night of the soul' of brief but incredible intensity; or it may be of many years' duration, for like other great spiritual ordeals, such as the sun dance of the Native Americans, it is a test of our inner strength and endurance.

There is good evidence that the monks of Glastonbury Abbey saw the Tor as a Hill of Purgatory and of Calvary, associating the place with the ultimate forms of spiritual testing and sacrifice. The Christian identification of 'this holyest erthe' with experiences of profound spiritual testing, and also with sacrifice, is reinforced by the legendary association of Glastonbury both with the Holy Grail and with the two cruets containing the blood and sweat of Christ. In these cases, the sets of symbols describe the higher forms of initiation. From the Christian point of view, this purgatorial process was repeated in the cruel execution of the last Abbot, Richard Whiting, and two fellow monks on the Tor. In this context the Avalonian Henry de Forest told the author Richard Leviton: "The crucifixion of Glastonbury needs to be complete, the devastation and misery of soul must be more heart-rending, and the experience of the rock-bottom of despair more absolute than elsewhere… So much depends on Glastonbury's final resurrection."[3] However, a geomantic and pagan analysis of the workings of the subtle energies of the island can offer further insights into the mysterious character of the Glastonbury Experience.

Elemental Guardians

For certainly our pagan ancestors, Saxon, Celtic as well as Neolithic, also saw the island as a place of initiation. The Neolithic peoples who made wooden trackways across the Somerset Levels nearby appear to have viewed the island as sacred, since they did not settle here. But it is now clear they visited it to observe and celebrate the changing patterns of the sky in relation to the hills of the island.[4] Its later visitors identified Glastonbury with key otherworldly locations, as the Isle of Glass (*Ynis Witrin*, the Welsh Caer Wydr), or the apple-isle of the blessed dead (Avalon). Here, they said, the dying King

Arthur was ferried, to be healed of his wounds by Morgan le Fay. Morgan is an aspect of the British death goddess who can appear in terrible form and must ultimately be related to the Gaelic Morrigan, the 'great queen' of the battlefield, the Otherworld and the dead.

When early Saxons created the town they called Glaestingaburgh, they left us a legend of Glastonbury's foundation that involved a sow, an animal sacred to the goddess of the dead, who led her swineherd many miles before finally stopping in Glastonbury beneath an apple-tree, traditional food of other-worldly spirits. Saxons as well as Celts may also have fuelled local legends about the Tor as home to Gwynn ap Nudd. This psychopomp, sometimes called a Faery King, is Celtic in origin, but he is the local leader of a seasonal procession that was very important in Saxon folklore. This is the Wild Hunt, 'Woden's (Odin's) Hunt' whose other leaders include Herne the Hunter, King Arthur, and the Faery Queen in one of her many aspects, such as Diana. The hunt is a riding forth of dead souls, guardian spirits of the land, and female and male shamans and deities.

The painful intensity of the 'Glastonbury Experience' can be more clearly understood through these myths. As an initiatory process, it corresponds to a quasi-shamanic journey whose final goal is paradise or the upper world. This journey must pass at some point through the lower world or underworld: this was the region where many different ancient cultures saw dead souls being purified, long before Christianity divided the lower world into Hell and Purgatory. For those following the path of initiation, however, the lower world journey can be undergone during physical incarnation, as the seeker knowingly or unknowingly is compelled to follow a much-travelled spiritual path, traversed by shamans since the earliest origins of mankind. We can view this intensive process of soul cleansing and rebalancing as work that is still overseen by the ancient, pre-Christian guardians of Glastonbury. These guardians may appear in different forms, but local pagan tradition sees them above all as a goddess and god of the dead, named for us in legend as Morgan le Fay and Gwynn ap Nudd.

Geomancy of Avalon

The Avalonian process of inner cleansing can also be understood geomantically, in terms of the nature and location of the island itself. Glastonbury is a highly distinctive 'island' in the plain or 'vale' of the Somerset Levels, surmounted by a powerful focus for elemental energy: the Tor. This swirling vortex of intensely charged elemental energies is more usually encountered in wilderness locations, remote from human habitation. There is a remarkable combination of earth and water in and around Glastonbury, but a lack of ancient rocks. Rather, the island is sealed from below by a layer of impervious clay, the Keuper Marl. It is indeed a sealed alchemical retort, in which all the rain that falls on the island either evaporates or enters the subterranean aquifer, while the waters of the other springs are not so deep and come from the top. The sealed system creates a powerful pressure cooker of elemental energy. This situation has not been helped by the stagnant nature of the waters around the original island since the beginning of drainage on the Levels. In geomantic terms, the yin energies of the surrounding water that once balanced the yang energies created by the point of focus of the Tor can no longer disperse its elemental charge. This may account for the cyclical intensification of inner pressure felt by those who live upon the island. According to this analysis, for its alchemical alembic to function most effectively, Glastonbury may have to be surrounded once again by water.

From a geomantic and pagan point of view, the peculiar character of the Glastonbury experience is also directly related to the volatile nature of the invisible neighbours on the island! For the elemental powers that gather in such vortical locations will never be entirely comfortable with constant human proximity. This elemental and spiritual taboo was honoured on the ancient island, for there was no stone (or permanent) settlement here until the 'Dark Age' settlement on the Tor and the early Saxon era. At the same time, such a powerful concentration of elemental powers will normally need to have regular periods of energetic release. In wilderness locations these episodes take the form of extreme weather patterns and other events that impact severely on the landscape, including flood, fire and earthquake (the medieval earthquake on the Tor was thus a natural expression of energetic release). Some of the intensity of the Glastonbury experience is seemingly due to the lack of opportunity for elemental 'eruptions' in the natural landscape of the island; instead, the energies seeking release create psychic storms or turbulence which engender considerable conflict among the local population, in addition to their impact on individual processes of soul-growth. We would therefore advise anyone struggling with an intense phase of their Glastonbury Experience to make regular offerings at key sites around the island, as a gesture of thanks to the local guardians—and an acknowledgement that we are walking on sacred ground.

So it is precisely what makes Glastonbury an *axis mundi*—a world mountain—that can also make it extremely uncomfortable in human terms! Instead of the tolerance that might be induced by a more varied landscape of multiple centres and features, supportive of spiritual pluralism and many different perspectives, the Tor as a 'hill of vision' can create an excessive singular inner focus. This was helpful perhaps to early monotheistic hermits and to disciplined monks, but it becomes problematic in a small human community not bound by a single spiritual code. It may sometimes feel that there is only room here for one point of view, one religion, one philosophy: that only one can stand on top of the world-mountain at a time. This distorting perspective may throw up a competitive, hostile attitude, separating those in the community instead of uniting them. It may have been a further reason for the decision of prehistoric peoples not to dwell upon the island. Once again, it is worth observing in this connection how Tibetan Buddhists approach their own sacred mountain, Mount Kailash: they do not set foot upon it, but laboriously circumambulate it, making many prayers and offerings to the mountain deity.

The Years Ahead

Between 2012 to 2014, transiting Pluto in Capricorn will exactly oppose the Sun-Jupiter conjunction in Glastonbury's town chart, while the same sensitive point will be squared by transiting Uranus in Aries. This is an indication that the 'Glastonbury Experience' is now intensifying, in connection with the unprecedented planetary emergency unfolding at this time. The invisible flame of spiritual intensity that heats the water in the alembic is being turned up, as it were, and the inner pressure is building, in elemental as well as human terms. We can all see this process happening across the planet, as the deeper effects and implications of our unsustainable society begin to impact upon humanity, through environmental and economic crises and already bitter resource wars.

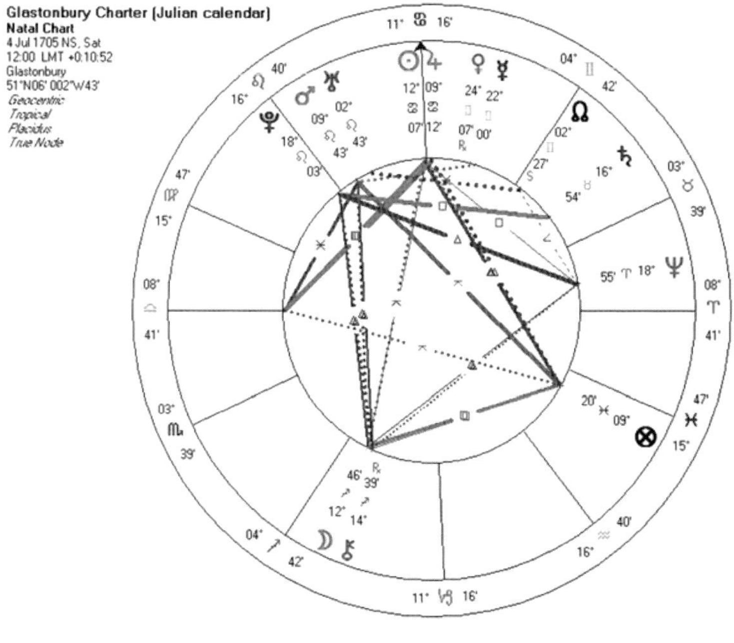

This chart for Glastonbury has been corrected to take account of the unadjusted English calendar, which in 1705 had still not been updated to conform to the more accurate Gregorian calendar. There was an 11 day difference between the two calendars.

Some on the path believe that the years leading up to 2012 represent a particular time of spiritual testing, and that some of the opportunities they afford for spiritual breakdown and breakthrough may become restricted after 2018.[5] The chances are that the initiatory process will not become any easier, and in certain respects it may become harder, as our dominant global culture, out of balance with life and caught up in staggering economic illusions, struggles to maintain its grip upon the self. Humanity may well fail its current collective initiation. We may fail to recoil in horror at what we are doing to the Earth. We may remain asleep in old patterns of behaviour, and refuse to face the inner shadows that are thrown up at this time, above all at powerful spiritual centres where the elemental powers are still strong. Yet if we can hear the outraged appeal of the elemental powers, as they demand that we honour and cooperate with them by living sustainably, we may be permitted to walk forward upon what the Native Americans call the Good Red Road—the balanced path of personal initiation and planetary transformation. For many of us, the access point to that path of higher consciousness will be through the gateway that is Glastonbury.

[1] There is a helpful account of the process of initiation in *Initiation, Human and Solar* (Lucis Trust, 1922), the first book channeled by Alice Bailey from the Master Dhjwal Khul.

[2] The concept of 'crossing the abyss' was central to the Kabbalistic teachings of the magical Order of the Golden Dawn, whose members included George Bernard Shaw, W B Yeats, Aleister Crowley and Dion Fortune.

[3] Richard Leviton, *Looking for Arthur: a once and future travelogue* (2nd edition, 2006).

[4] See Mann and Glasson, *The Star Temple of Avalon: Glastonbury's ancient observatory revealed* (Temple Publications, 2007).

[5] This chart is based on the Town charter awarded to Glastonbury by Queen Anne on June 23rd 1705.

Bibliography

Abraham, Lyndy, 1998, *A Dictionary of Alchemical Imagery*, Cambridge University Press.
Ashe, Geoffrey: (1) 1968 (editor), *The Quest for Arthur's Britain*, Paladin. (2) 1979, *The Glastonbury Tor Maze*, Gothic Image.
Benham, Patrick 1993, *The Avalonians*, Gothic Image.
Dowman, Keith, 1984, *Sky Dancer: The Secret life and Songs of the Lady Yeshe Tsogyel,* Routledge & Kegan Paul.
Fabricius, Johannes, 1976, *Alchemy*, Rosenkilde and Bagger.
French, Peter, 1972, *John Dee: The World of an Elizabethan Magus*, Routledge & Kegan Paul.
Geoffrey of Monmouth, *The History of the Kings of Britain,* trans., L. Thorpe, Penguin, 1966.
'Life of Gildas' and 'Life of St. Collen' in S. Baring-Gould & J. Fisher, *Lives of the British Saints*, 1911.
Giraldus Cambrensis, *The Historical Works*, trans., T. Wright & G. Bohn, 1863.
The Mabinogion, trans., J. Gantz, Penguin, 1976.
Harpur, Patrick, 2002, *The Philosophers' Secret Fire: A History of the Imagination*, Penguin.
Jung, C. G., 1953, *Psychology and Alchemy*, Routledge & Kegan Paul.
Klossowski de Rola, Stanislas, 1973, *Alchemy: The Secret Art*, Thames & Hudson.
Mann, Nicholas R., (1) 1985, *The Cauldron and the Grail*, Triskele. (2) 1986, 1993, *Glastonbury Tor*, Triskele. (3) 2001, *The Isle of Avalon*, Green Magic. (4) 2004, *Energy Secrets of Glastonbury Tor*, Green Magic.
Mann, Nicholas & Philippa Glasson, 2009, *The Star Temple of Avalon: Glastonbury's Ancient Observatory Revealed*, Temple Publications.
Marrin, West, 2002, *Universal Water: The Ancient Wisdom and Scientific Theory of Water*, Inner Ocean.
Matthews, Benjamin, 1751, *The Virtues and Efficacy of the Water of Glastonbury*, London, (Somerset Studies Library, Taunton).
Rahtz, Philip (1) 1964, *Excavations at Chalice Well, Glastonbury*, P.S.A.N.H.S. Vol. 108, pp145-163. (2) 1971, *Excavations on Glastonbury Tor, Somerset, 1964-6*, R.A.I. (4) 1993, *Glastonbury*, English Heritage.
Schwenk, Theodor (1) 1965, *Sensitive Chaos: The Creation of Flowing Forms in Water and Air*, Steiner Press. (2) 1989, *Water: The Element of Life*, Anthropomorphic Press.
Spess, David L., 2000, *Soma: the Divine Hallucinogen*, Park Street Press.
Tudor Pole, Wellesley, (1) 1965, *A Man Seen Afar*, Neville Spearman. (2) 1968, *Writing on the Ground*, Neville Spearman.
Wright, George W. (1) 1870, *The Chalice Well, or Blood Spring, and its Traditions*, Glastonbury Antiquarian Society Publication 1. (2) 1894, 'The History of Glastonbury During the Last Forty Years' *Bulleids of Glastonbury*, A. Goodall.

Some other books from The Temple Publications

Glastonbury Tor
Nicholas R. Mann

This best-selling guide draws a full picture of the mysterious landmark Glastonbury Tor. It describes the Monastery of St. Michael, the labyrinth, the astronomical alignments, the underground water, the geology, and the associated myths and legends. It sets the Tor in its various historic and prehistoric contexts to answer the question of the purpose behind the construction of the terraces.

Gwyn- Ancient God of Glastonbury and key to the Glastonbury Zodiac
Yuri Leitch

Leitch's new book explores Glastonbury's mysteries through its most ancient god, Gwyn ap Nudd, a figure who has been debased to a mere 'King of the Fairies'. The author draws back the curtain of time to restore Gwyn to his rightful place at the apex of the ancient British pantheon and reveals how he is fundamental to the landscape enigma that is the Glastonbury Zodiac.

The God Kings of England
Hugh Montgomery

The *God Kings* reveals how a struggle between two rival Dark Age dynasties, the Norse Ulvungar family and the Anglo- Saxon Odynic family, is central to the subsequent course of both English and world history. At stake in this titanic clash were the nature of Christianity and ultimately the very soul of western civilization.

Royston Cave- Used by Saints or Sinners?
Sylvia Beamon

Beneath the streets of Royston lies a secret! A man made cave engraved with religious (Christian, pagan and Masonic) symbolism that has confounded and mesmerised in equal measure since its rediscovery in 1742. This book puts this unique creation into historical context through comparison with carvings and graffiti found elsewhere in Britain and Europe and ruminates upon the real nature and purpose of this most magical of structures.

What Wise Men Do - The Secret World of Conan Doyle, Bram Stoker, Jules Verne and the Unseen Hand

Philip Gardiner

What Wise Men Do takes the reader on a journey to uncover the real purpose, until now hidden, of some of history's great physicians, politicians and writers. This is a controversial but always compelling re-analysis of history told from the point of view of one of today's most prolific alternative authors.

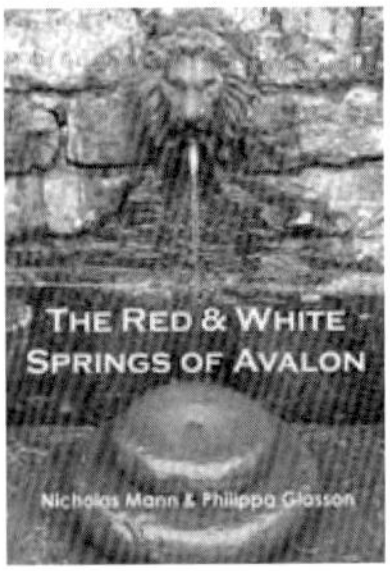

The Star Temple of Avalon -
Glastonbury's Ancient Observatory Revealed

Nicholas R Mann & Philippa Glasson

The Star Temple of Avalon represents a groundbreaking study providing decisive proof for the existence of a Neolithic astronomical observatory at Glastonbury, the legendary Isle of Avalon. By highlighting the intimate relationship between Glastonbury's holy hills and pathways with the courses of the sun, moon and stars, the authors reveal the full spiritual potency of one of the worlds most magical locations.

Before the Delusion -
Secret Vatican Files of the Pyramids and Stonehenge

William Gleeson

A radically different historical novel of ancient Egypt, impressively re-searched from ancient sources suppressed by the Church. Compelling new translations reveal the true function of the pyramids – and the origin of the men who migrated west to emboss their history in the megaliths of Carnac, Newgrange and Stonehenge. Disturbingly plausible.

The Temple # 14

Ed. Oddvar Olsen

The Temple is a quarterly periodical dedicated to providing a platform for original articles pertaining to the Knights Templar and related subjects, such as the Grail/ Arthurian Legends, Masonic Lore, Early Christianity, Alchemy and much more. Since its inception in 2002 the Temple has been at the cutting edge of research into these subjects and has published articles by both renowned authors as well as so called coffee-table students.

www.thetemplepublications.co.uk
Info@thetemplepublications.co.uk

The Red & White Springs of Avalon

All over the British Isles natural springs appear. Many are regarded as holy and are reputed to possess healing properties. Among the most venerated of these healing waters are the Red and White Springs that flow from the base of the famed Glastonbury Tor.

In *The Red & White Springs of Avalon* the authors draw on alchemy and other spiritual traditions to explain the hidden powers of these two remarkable springs. They show how these ancient wisdom traditions provide important keys to the initiatory and healing secrets of Avalon. This fascinating exploration of Chalice Well, the Tor and the White Spring has become an essential guide to the mysteries of Glastonbury.

Geomancer **Nicholas R. Mann** B.A. is the author of *Glastonbury Tor, The Isle of Avalon, Energy Secrets of Glastonbury Tor, Druid Magic, The Silver Branch Cards* and *The Sacred Geometry of Washington DC*. **Philippa Glasson** D.Phil. is an astrologer and seer who taught in the University of Cambridge for many years. She is the author of influential books and articles on subjects ranging from Renaissance alchemy to postmodern spirituality. Nicholas and Philippa are the joint authors of *The Star Temple of Avalon.*

The Temple Publications